D0328194

THE GREATEST PASSAGES OF THE BIBLE

20 SERMONS ON GOD'S MOST IMPORTANT MESSAGES

Robert L. Allen

C.S.S. Publishing Co., Inc.

Lima, Ohio

THE GREATEST PASSAGES OF THE BIBLE

Library of Congress Cataloging-in-Publication Data

Allen, Robert L., 1946-
    The Greatest Passages of the Bible: twenty sermons on God's most important messages / by Robert L. Allen
        p. cm.
    ISBN 1-55673-172-8
    1. Sermons, American. 2. United Methodist Church (U.S.) — Sermons.
3. Methodist Church — Sermons. 4. Bible — Sermons. I. Title.
BX8333.A1A44 1990   252'.076 — dc20   89-27605
ISBN 1-55673-172-8

9019 / ISBN 1-55673-172-8   PRINTED IN U.S.A.

This book is dedicated to
my wife Madalyne and our two children,
Jennifer and Jeff

Table of Contents

Preface

The Bible is made up of sixty-six different books. There are thirty-nine books in the Old Testament and twenty-seven books in the New Testament. These books were written by over 100 different people. Most likely, the writers did not think in terms of writing Holy Scripture. They were simply telling the story of God's love by relating the history of Israel or writing biographies of people of faith. They told the story in poetry and wisdom literature . . . They told the story in relating the laws and legends of the people of God . . . They told the story in the letters of the apostles and apocalyptic literature . . .

I realize that any attempt to select the greatest passages in the Bible is purely subjective. The passages which one person selects would not be the same passages which another would choose. There are so many great passages in the Bible that it is almost impossible to choose only twenty passages and call them the greatest passages in the Bible. Nevertheless, this book takes several of the greatest passages in the Bible and attempts to sum up the messages. In these chapters, we attempt to cover all of the major themes of the Bible — the existence of God . . . the destructive reality of sin . . . the birth of the Savior . . . the power of prayer . . . the crucifixion of Jesus . . . the resurrection of Christ . . . and the love of God for all people . . .

As you read through these chapters, it is my hope that the central message of God's love will become a reality to you.

Robert L. Allen

In The Beginning

Walter de la Mare wrote a fascinating little poem entitled, "The Listeners." He wrote:

> *"Is anybody there?" asked the Traveler,*
> *Knocking on the moonlight door;*
> *And his horse in the silence chomped the grasses*
> *Of the forest's ferny floor;*
> *And a bird flew up out of the turret,*
> *Above the traveler's head:*
> *And he smote upon the door again a second time;*
> *"Is anybody there?" he said.*
> *But no one descended to the traveler;*
> *No head from the leaf-fringed sill*
> *Leaned over and looked into his gray eyes,*
> *Where he stood perplexed and still.*

Is anybody there? This is one of the long, agonizing questions of the ages when people have looked to the heavens and wondered about God. Thousands and thousands of people have stood in the silence and asked, "Is there anybody there?" If there is a God, where is he?

The asking of that question has led to many answers. Some have asked the question and come back with a wishful agnosticism. They say we really can't answer the question of God. Robert Ingersoll stood at the grave of his brother and said:

> *Life is a narrow veil between the cold and barren peaks*
> *of two eternities. We strive to look beyond their heights.*

9

We cry aloud, and the only answer is the echo of our wailing cry. But hope sees a star, and in the night of death, listening love can hear the rustling of an angel's wing.

Some have asked the question, "Is there anybody there?" and they have come back with a bitter atheism — a bitter denial of God. Jean Paul Richter said:

I have traveled the world, I have risen to the suns. There is no God! I have gazed into the gulf beyond and cried out, 'Where art Thou?' And no answer came. We are utterly alone.

And others have asked the question and come back with an awesome vision of power, but a power so remote and so uninterested in his creation that he has forgotten us. Mark Twain, the great American writer, used to say:

Special Providence! Why the phrase nauseates me. God doesn't know where we are and wouldn't care if He did.

There are times in our lives when we wonder the same things. In spite of the hymns of faith that we sing...in spite of the creeds we repeat affirming our belief in God...in spite of the prayers we send up to the heavens...there are times when God just doesn't seem to be around. One of the popes of the Catholic church, Pope Julian, knew this feeling when he said: "When I pray, God seems to be deaf."

I have been a minister for several years and I have pastored three different churches. During this time, I have been with parents when a child died...I have gone into homes to tell families that a loved one has been killed in an accident...I have sat and prayed with families as illness claimed the life of one they loved. All of these people, in one way or another, have asked, "Is anybody there? If God is real, why doesn't he do something? Why doesn't he prove he exists?"

I can understand the agony and grief which produces these questions. We are hurting...we are grieving...and like the traveler in the poem, we want to know if anybody is up there in the heavens. We want to prove that he is God.

However, you can't read very far into the Bible without getting the idea that there is no attempt to prove God. The first verse begins with the assumption of God. It says:

"In the beginning, God created the heavens and the earth . . ."

The Bible doesn't waste time trying to prove the existence of anyone being out there; it simply begins with the obvious.

There is an old story about a boy who believed that the blue sky was just a big blue tent. When he went to school, he learned that the sky was not a big blue tent. He reported to his friends, "There ain't no sky."

One of the boys tilted his head back and looked at the clouds. He looked at the sun shining brightly, he looked at the beautiful blue sky that went from one horizon to another, then he asked, "What is it that ain't?"

Although the boy's grammar may not have been very good, it was a good question. Something was obviously there! And so it is with the question of God. We cannot find God and prove God...we can't put God into some test tube and analyze him. It is like your love for someone. Your love is seen by what you do...by what you say...by how you live. And it is the same with God! The Bible simply assumes the obvious, "God is..." and we see the evidence of his presence. Next I want to look at a couple ways we can see his presence.

I. We see his presence in the steady, unfailing order of creation. The faithfulness of God is consistent. Each day the sun shines and each night the stars sparkle across the darkened sky. There is an orderliness to this universe that even the Psalmist of over 2500 years ago could see when he wrote, "...I consider thy heavens, the work of thy fingers, the moon and the stars, which thou hast ordained..." (Psalm 8) When we look at this universe in all of its magnitude and the atom in all of its infinitesimal perfection, we begin to grasp the greatness and orderliness of God in creation.

I was fascinated a while back because something very small, yet very significant took place. A computer system that is so precise and so accurate that it would take 300 years to be two -fifths of a second off in time told our scientists that we needed to add one second to a year. So, at precisely midnight of January 1, 1988, the scientists at Greenwich, England, added one second to that year.

The thing which caught my attention was not the computer which told us to add one second to our year. What I wondered was how the computer knew. And the answer was simple. The computer tested itself against another, more precise clock — the universe itself. The computer, keeping track of the movement of the earth and moon and planets and stars, could accurately tell us we needed to add one more second to our clocks that year.

I don't see how we can miss this evidence...this awareness of the presence of God. When Jesus preached, he often used the world around him to make a point of God's presence. He said that no flower ever bloomed that was not nourished by God's care; he said that no sparrow ever fell to the ground without God being aware; he said that God knows so much about you and me that even the hairs of our head are numbered.

God's love and faithfulness is so constant that we have a tendency to take it for granted and to forget the deeper faith. Perhaps the very constancy of God's creation dims our gratitude. Because the sun shines each day, we scarely notice it; because the seasons come with regularity — spring, summer, autumn, and winter — we seem more impressed with a large snowfall than by the abiding constancy that January is always a cold month. We have a tendency to look for God in the spectacular and the unusual; and we miss him in the constant, everyday order of things which confirms that he is so near. How near is God? God is...

As near as green grass is to a hill
As petals of gold to a daffodil,
As near as the sunlight is to the sod,
So near to the human heart is God.

II. *We see his presence in the midst of his people.* The evidence of God is not only visible in the steady, unfailing order of creation, but he is here among us, working out his will, and moving toward his eternal purpose in our midst. God is not an absentee landlord, but he is here among us.

During World War I, a war that was fought in muddy trenches, a young British soldier was close to mental breakdown. The artillery bombardment...the stench of death...the fear, they had driven him to the point of despair. He looked at his captain and asked, "Sir, you said you believed in God. Where is God in all of this?"

Just then, two stretcher-bearers climed over the top of the trench and moved out under enemy fire to pick up a wounded soldier lying in no-mans-land. And the Captain said, "Look, private, there goes God now."

God is not a spectator looking on from the heavens. God is all of our efforts to bring light out of darkness; God is in every deed of compassion; God is in every act of mercy shown; God is in our hospitals where doctors and nurses minister to those who are sick; God is in every court of law trying to bring justice and righteousness; God is in every human endeavor where kindness and forgiveness are shown; God is in all the events of our time, and we need to constantly remind ourselves that there is something at work in history that is beyond us — and that the destiny of the world is in stronger hands than ours.

When President Reagan and the Soviet leader, General Secretary Gorbachev, signed the peace treaty to begin destroying part of their stockpile of nuclear weapons, there was a cartoon in a religious magazine that made a profound point. The cartoon pictured the angel Gabriel, up in heaven, about to blow his horn and end life on this planet. But God, looking down on this earth said, "Hold on, Gabriel. They're going to have another peace conference."

Where is God? He is here in our midst. He is in the conference which move nations toward peace...He is in the work of missionaries who cross the seas to serve him...He is in your daily lives as you cross the street to help a neighbor or to be a friend to someone in need.

I realize that it is not very spectacular and it won't make the front pages of the paper, but it tells us where God is. He is here. He is among his people. He is becoming known by the way we, his followers. live our lives every day.

III. We see his presence in Jesus Christ.

If you want to see the clearest evidence of God, you will not find it by looking to the heavens; you will not find it in the realm of nature; you will not find it in the goodness of humanity. The clearest word of God was made flesh and lived among us in the person of Jesus Christ. He is the heart, mind, and nature of God spelled out in the language of life.

If you want to see the clearest evidence of God, look to Jesus Christ who was born in a stable in Bethlehem...If you want to see the clearest evidence of God, look to Jesus Christ who was crucified on a Roman cross saying, "God is like this. God is like I am." If you want the clearest evidence of God, look to Jesus Christ who walked forth from the tomb because death could not hold him.

The clearest word of God has been made known to us in Jesus Christ. You can open up your life to him and depend on him forever.

Will you?

The Reality Of Sin

Genesis 3:1-13

Someone once asked me, "Where was the Garden of Eden located?"

I looked at him and said, "The Garden of Eden was located at 803 Blue Street in Hope, Arkansas."

A surprised look crossed this man's face. For a moment he was speechless and then he asked, "Arkansas? I thought the Garden of Eden was supposed to have been someplace in the Middle East."

"Well," I responded, "I don't really know where the biblical Garden of Eden was located. But, I know that my Garden of Eden was on Blue Street in Hope, Arkansas. I was only a young boy (four or five years old) and I did something that I knew was wrong. My father usually put his change in a caddy on his dresser. I took a quarter without asking and went down to the store and bought myself some candy. As I ate the candy, shame overwhelmed me, guilt gripped at my heart, and sin became a reality for the first time in my life. My Garden of Eden was lost and I was embarrassed by my sinfulness. The lush, secure world of a little boy had evaporated and I headed home from the store aware that what I had done was wrong. Sin was no longer something only found in Bible stories. Sin was now a reality in my life."

This third chapter of Genesis is the story of sin becoming a reality to humanity. This story of Adam and Eve and the Garden of Eden is one of the best known passages in all of the Bible. It was written at least 500 years before the birth of

Jesus and it is a story which attempts to explain how sin and evil came into the world.

According to the story, everything was good in the beginning. Adam and Eve had everything they desired because God controlled everything and no one had any problems. One day they decided to eat the forbidden fruit of a certain tree. There is no word in the Bible about it being an apple tree — just a tree whose fruit they were forbidden to eat.

The lure of that which is forbidden seems to be the most tempting. So they ate of the forbidden fruit. First Eve took a bite and then Adam. Suddenly, they felt guilty; suddenly, they felt ashamed; suddenly, sin became a reality to them. Now they were afraid and they tried to hide themselves from God. But, how do you hide from God? The voice of God came to Adam asking, "Where are you, Adam?"

And Adam replied, "I was afraid and tried to hide."

God asked, "Why did you try to hide? Did you eat of the fruit from which I told you not to eat?"

And Adam answered with an excuse, "It wasn't my fault. This woman you gave me to be my wife told me to eat the fruit." (I have a feeling that their honeymoon was over that very minute.)

Then God turned to Eve and asked, "Eve, why did you do this?"

I love Eve's response. She said, "Lord, it's really not my fault either. It's the snake's fault."

I suppose that everyone has tried to lay their blame on others. But, Adam and Eve knew where to place the blame. You can't point a finger at someone else without pointing three fingers at yourself. Adam and Eve were confronted with the reality of their sin.

Like Adam and Eve, we have all been confronted with the reality of our sins. We know what it is to feel guilty . . . We know what it is to be caught off-base and to be embarrassed...We know what it is to come up short of what we expect of ourselves...We know what it is to do things that are wrong, not get caught, and then have to live with it, whatever the frustrations might be. Sin is not simply something from biblical times. Every last one of us is confronted each day with the reality of our sins. We are not sinners simply because Adam sinned. We were not born into sin. We are sinners, because, like Adam and Eve, we have rebelled in our own hearts and minds against God.

As we look at the reality of sin, there are three things which are important in dealing with the idea of sin in the present tense. *I. There is sin in our world.* If we were to set aside the lessons we learn from the Bible and simply look at life in our world, we would be aware of the reality of sin. A simple walk down the streets of our city should convince us of the reality of sin. After many robberies and assaults on the elderly of our country, there are many people trapped by fear in their own homes; crosses found burning in the yards of homes and churches are vivid testimonies that racism still lingers in the hearts of many; the swastikas and anti-semitic slogans painted on Jewish temples and synagogues give witness to the bigotry and hatred which dwells in our world.

There are thousands of men and women who never read the Bible and don't have the foggiest notion of what it teaches about sin. But, in their everyday relationships, they live and move and run their lives on the assumption that sin is in our world. That's why a loan officer at a bank checks your credit rating...That's why we spent several thousand dollars installing a security system to protect our church against thieves . . . That's why at this very moment the keys to your car are in your pocket or purse. We may not be theologically trained, but we are theologically conditioned. We may not read the

Bible, but we have read human nature and we are under no illusions about the reality of sin in our world.

Many of us were shocked with the news of nine-year-old Darlwin Carlisle being found in an abandoned house in Gary, Indiana. Apparently, she was found locked in the unheated attic of an abandoned house. Doctors said that her frostbitten legs were so damaged after being in the extreme cold for five days that they would have to amputate both legs.

The girl's mother was on drugs and she had simply abandoned the little girl in her search for a fix. Her concern was not for a nine-year-old daughter who needed her, but for a drug-induced high which would black out the reality of the world.

I don't suppose there are many sins in our world which are more pervasive than the use of drugs. The illegal use of drugs accounts for a majority of the crime in our nation...and fills our prisons...and claims the lives of many each year. But, the use of drugs is only the tip of the iceberg. There are so many other sins which have an impact on our world. The industrialization which pollutes our water and destroys the ozone layer of our atmosphere...the hundred little wars which rage around the world...the existence of the homeless who live on our streets and exist from day to day, and the litany could go on and on.

Whether we read the Bible or not, sin is the most realistic fact in our world. Sin is real, and every day, we are confronted with its tragic consequences in our midst.

II. There is sin in our lives. All of us certainly know what it is to sin. The Apostle Paul said, *"I don't do the good that I want to do; instead, I do the evil that I do not want to do . . ." (Romans 7:19)* This is not merely one man's confession, but it is the confession within each of our hearts. There is something of the saint and something of the sinner in each of our lives.

19

There is an old story about a little boy who was standing in front of a display counter of candy. He had that "Boy, I'd like some candy look" on his face. But, he didn't have any money. The manager walked by, smiled at the boy, and asked, "Are you trying to make up your mind which candy bar you want?"

"No sir," said the boy. "I'm trying to make up my mind not to take one and run."

We know something of the struggle of that little boy. We know of these struggles within to take the lower road instead of the higher road . . . We know of the struggle with right and wrong . . . We know of the struggle with sin in our lives . . . We are all guilty and we know it.

There once was a stern-faced, plainly dressed man who could be seen standing on a busy street corner in the heart of the city. As pedestrians hurried by on their way to lunch and business appointments, he would solemnly lift his right arm, . . . point to the nearest person and loudly yell, "Guilty!"

Then, without any change of expression, he would resume his stiff stance for a few moments before repeating the gesture. Then, again, he would raise his arm, again he would point at the nearest person, and again he would yell, "Guilty!"

The effect of this strange pantomime on the unsuspecting pedestrians was extraordinary. They would stop in their tracks, they would stare at the man, they would hesitate for a moment, they would look to see if he was, perhaps, pointing at someone else, they would look at the strange man one more time, then they would hurry on their ways.

One man, who had been singled out, turned to his companion and asked, "But, how did he know?"

"Guilty! Everyone is guilty," is what this strange man on a busy street corner seemed to be saying. And so we are! We are guilty of sin and we know it. We have struggled with right and wrong and we know that there have been times when we have given in to sin. We know the reality of sin in our lives.

And that brings us to my last point about the reality of sin. *III. There is forgiveness of sins.* Either your sin is forgiven or else it is in you still as sin. That is a fact of human life. There is no peace in our lives until our sins are forgiven.

In that great novel, *The Scarlet Letter*, Arthur Dimmesdale fathered the child of a young woman. In that culture, she became an outcast of society and was branded with the scarlet letter ''A'' — for adulteress. She would not reveal who the father of the child was and Arthur Dimmesdale seemed to get off completely free.

But did he? His unconfessed, unforgiven sin plagued him with guilt. How was he to get rid of the guilt? He was a man of intellect; he would absorb himself in study — but, that was no way out. He was a minister; he would preach sermons and save souls — but that was no way out. He was a servant and would go from door to door, humbly helping people — but that was no way out. There was only one way for Arthur Dimmesdale to escape the guilt of his unconfessed sin and that was to confess his sin and seek forgiveness.

And when you look at your own life, you know this to be true. Either you have confessed your sin and been forgiven or else your sin is still in you.

You can forget about your sins for a little while, you can lock them out of your conscious mind and believe they are forgotten, you can let the roar of the world drown out the still small voice of conscience for a short, short period. But, sooner or later, that unforgiven sin will resurface to haunt us . . . to embarrass us . . . to fill us with guilt. Many of us have unforgiven sins buried within. The challenge is to unlock that hidden door in our consciences, reach that secret place and pull out the unforgiven sins, and lay it at the Cross of Jesus Christ saying, ''O God have mercy on me, a sinner.''

Rules For Living

Exodus 20:1-17

A couple of years ago, I was asked to serve on a panel to discuss the problems facing teenagers in our society. The panel included a school counselor, a Juvenile Judge, a drug counselor, a couple of other experts on teenage problems, and, I guess, I was the representative of the religious community.

There were a variety of people in the audience, including the parents of several teenagers. During the question and answer period, there was one woman who acknowledged that she was at the symposium because her adolescent daughter had become a handful and she could no longer control her. Then, looking at me, she began to blame the church for the problems that her daughter faced and the problems that teenagers were encountering in our society. She stated that the problems of teenagers could be traced directly to the church which was no longer teaching "the basics." She talked about the failure of the church to give proper instruction and moral guidance to the younger generation. Her strongest and most self-evident point was that children were no longer required to memorize the Ten Commandments.

Finally, when she had finished listing her complaints, I asked her, "Madam, do you know the Ten Commandments?"

"Of course," she responded, somewhat insulted by the question.

Looking directly at this woman in the audience, I challenged her by saying, "Name them!"

She coughed and sputtered and looked embarrassed. Finally, she was able to name three or four of the commandments

22

and a couple of quotes from Shakespeare before giving up and sitting down.

While I can sympathize with that woman and her worry about her daughter, I think it is a mistake to attribute magical qualities to the Ten Commandments. Instead, I think it is more appropriate to look at them as rules for living.

The Jewish people did not need to make their own rules when they were in Egypt. They were too busy trying to survive the bondage of their Egyptian taskmasters. They were too busy trying to keep the many rules given to them by the Egyptians. They were too busy working as slaves in Egypt to worry about any rules for living. But, then Moses led them out of Egypt and toward the Promised Land. Once they were on the road to freedom, they needed their own rules and regulations. A society without rules and regulations has to create them.

So, while the Hebrew people were in the wilderness, Moses went up on Mt. Sinai. When he came down from the mountain, he brought the Ten Commandments to the people. Some of these commandments can be found in other cultures and other societies. However, this was the first time these particular Ten Commandments were brought together. Moses brought these rules for living down from the mountain for the Children of Israel. But, these commandments are not restricted just to the Hebrew people. These rules for living are for all peoples and for all times. They are rules that will never go out of date; they are rules that will never be repealed; they are rules that will never change; they are rules which will never budge because they are eternally the same.

These rules for living that Moses brought down from Mt. Sinai are called the Ten Commandments. As we look at these rules for living, it is worth noting that the first four deal with our relationship to God, and the last six deal with our relationship to other people. Before any of us can live rightly, we must have some principles within which to guide our lives.

In these rules for living, there are three things which I believe are important.

I. The Ten Commandments deal with our relationship to God. The first four commandments clearly deal with our relationship to God. The first commandment affirms the supremacy of God by declaring, "You shall have no other gods before me." The second commandment declares the dangers of worshipping gods that we make when it says, "You shall not make for yourself a graven image." The third commandment forbids the reckless use of the name of God in promises, pledges, and vows when it declares, "You shall not take the name of the Lord your God in vain." And the fourth commandment reminds us of the sacredness of the Sabbath when we have the opportunity of turning our thoughts toward God. This commandment challenges us to "remember the Sabbath and keep it holy."

Through these commandments, God was calling his people back then and today — to share a covenant relationship with him. This covenant relationship simply means that we learn to give God a prominent place in our lives.

Not long ago, I was reading a book about the presidency of Jimmy Carter. He was the Democratic president of the United States from January 1977 to January 1981. During that time he dealt with many difficult issues. He was nominated for the Nobel Peace Prize in his efforts to bring peace between Israel and Egypt. He dealt with an oil embargo crisis and the crisis of the hostages in Iran. But, one thing that Jimmy Carter will be remembered for is the influence of his religion in his life.

Once, he was being interviewed by Bill Moyers, who looked at the new President of the United States of America and asked, "What is the most significant discovery Jimmy Carter has made?"

President Carter flashed his famous smile and said, "This is embarrassing a little bit for me to talk about because it's personal. But, the most significant discovery that I have made is my relationship with God through Jesus Christ."

He was the most powerful man in the free world. Every day he made decisions that affected the destiny of our nation and the world. He was busy as he sought to move our country in a new direction. Yet, he had his priorities straight, because he recognized that his relationship with God was the most significant part of his life.

Are you putting God first in your life?

Have you learned the importance of developing a relationship to God in your life?

When you learn the importance of a relationship with God through Jesus Christ, you will have learned a rule that gives real meaning to your life.

II. *The Ten Commandments deal with our relationships with other people.* When we look at the next six commandments, it is clear that they deal with relationships with other people. The fifth commandment affirms the importance of the home when it challenges us to "honor our father and mother." The sixth commandment speaks of the sacredness of human life when it states, "You shall not kill." The seventh commandment affirms the sacredness of marriage when it declares, "You shall not commit adultery." The eighth commandment cautions us against the temptation of taking what is not ours when it says, "You shall not steal." The ninth commandment demands that we live by truth when it declares, "You shall not bear false witness against your neighbor." And the tenth commandment warns of the peril of greed when it states, "You shall not covet."

These commandments make sense because they clearly spell out how we are to relate to people. We are challenged to learn to love other people. In fact, Jesus put it very clearly when he said, " . . . love your neighbor as yourself."

This is a revolutionary concept. Our relationships with other people are first, last, and always vitally important. We are to love other people and care about other people simply because they are God's children. After all, how can we claim to have a relationship with God unless we are willing to develop a caring relationship with his people?

Recently, I read a little fable about a young girl who was walking through a meadow. She saw that a beautiful butterfly had one wing impaled by a thorn. Very carefully, so as not to further damage the wing, she released the butterfly from the thorn and it began to fly away.

Then, the butterfly came back and changed into a beautiful fairy princess right before the little girl. "For your kindness," the fairy told the little girl, "I will grant you your fondest wish."

The little girl thought for a moment and replied, "I want to be happy."

The fairy princess smiled and leaned over and whispered something into the girl's ear. Then, the fairy princess vanished into thin air. But, as the girl grew older, there was no one in the kingdom who was happier than she. Whenever anyone asked her for the secret of her happiness, she would only smile and say, "I listened to a beautiful fairy princess."

As she reached the last years of her life, her friends and neighbors were afraid that her fabulous secret of happiness would die with her. "Tell us, please," they asked. "Tell us what the fairy said!"

The little girl, who was now a lovely old lady, smiled and said, "The beautiful fairy princess told me that the secret to happiness is to realize that everyone, no matter how secure they seem, has need of me."

One of the great secrets of life is to realize that everyone has need of us. And the willingness to give ourselves to others . . . the willingness to develop a relationship with others . . . the willingness to love others, is one of the rules of living which leads to a happy life.

III. The Ten Commandments deal with our ethics for life. When you look at the Ten Commandments as a whole, they are not simply a group of rules and regulations. They are a series of principles which attempt to define an ethical standard for life. You shall not steal . . . You shall not kill . . . You shall not build idols . . . You shall not commit adultry . . . Honor your father and your mother.

The Ten Commandments attempt to tell us that to be human is to be responsible. They attempt to provide a series of principles or ethics for life which affirm that there are some things that are right and some things that are wrong.

We live in a world where old standards of morality are being questioned. We live in a world where some have abandoned the idea of fairness and replaced it with the goal of winning, even if we have to lie and cheat and steal in order to win. We live in a world that is caught in a whirlpool of change — and concern for the have-nots and helpless people of our society has been replaced with our own selfish desires "to make it" no matter what it costs.

Into this world of upheaval and change, the Ten Commandments still ring true. Close to 3,000 years have come and gone since Moses came down from Mt. Sinai. He carried with him Ten Commandments for living, not Ten Suggestions. These Ten Commandments have not budged one inch in calling men and women to the same ethical standards of life. Times may have changed, but the principles of these Ten Commandments are eternally the same.

Lloyd Douglas told how he loved, occasionally, to visit a little old man who gave violin lessons. He had a studio, if it could be called that, a small room set in a long row of rooms where other music teachers taught.

"I liked to drop in on him," Douglas said, "for he had a kind of homely wisdom that refreshed me. One morning I walked in and by way of greeting, said, 'Well, what's the good news for today?' "

Putting down his violin, stepping over to his tuning fork suspended from a silk thread, he struck it a sharp blow with a padded mallet, and said, "There is the good news for today. That, my friend, is 'A.' It was 'A' all day yesterday . . . it will be 'A' all day tomorrow, next week, and for a thousand years . . . the soprano upstairs warbles off-key . . . the tenor next door flats his high ones . . . the piano across the hall is out of tune . . . noise all around me, noise . . . noise . . . noise; but that, my friend, is 'A.' "

I believe it will steady your soul to remember that. Some things remain constant in the midst of noise and change . . . some things are not transient . . . some things are not at the mercy of popular vote . . . some things, like the Ten Commandments, are timeless and permanent! You can come back to them and confidently follow them with your life. They are rules or guidelines for living that come to us from God.

Are you following his guidelines for living?

The Lord Is My Shepherd

Psalm 23

We were just completing our evening meal when the phone rang. The kids started laughing because the joke around our house is that we cannot sit down to eat without the phone ringing just once. Sometimes it is someone trying to sell us siding for the house . . . or it's a phone call for one of the kids . . . or a phone call from someone just to chat. On this night, the call was to let me know that Bob had taken a turn for the worse. A family member was calling and asking if I could come to the hospital. I slipped a jacket on and headed toward the hospital.

As I drove to the hospital, I thought about the man I was going to visit. Bob had unusual abilities and energies. He had started working with one company, but eventually formed his own company and became very successful. Perhaps, it was that drive and determination which led him to a heart attack at the age of fifty-two.

When I arrived at the hospital, the doctor was telling the family that the situation was not good. Bob was in serious condition, he was no longer awake or alert and his condition was deteriorating. I walked into that room with the family and as we stood around the bed, Bob's wife was holding my hand and she asked me if I would say a word of prayer. We all joined hands and bowed our heads. For some reason, instead of saying a prayer, I simply began repeating the best known passage in the Bible. I said:

The Lord is my shepherd:
I shall not want.

He maketh me to lie down in green pastures;
He leadeth me beside the still waters . . .

Somehow, those words were reaching into the heart and mind of Bob. Even though his eyes were still closed and the heart monitor indicated that he was growing progressively weaker, he began to repeat that Psalm with me. His voice was weak, but there was no doubt that he knew that Psalm.

The Twenty-third Psalm is one of the most powerful pieces of writing in existence. For twenty-five centuries, it has crossed the barriers of time, language, and culture to become one of the best-known and most-loved passages in the Bible. All who read this Psalm discover a quiet beauty of thought. It is a Psalm of spiritual insight. It is a Psalm which breathes confidence and trust in the Lord.

Scholars occasionally wonder if and when David wrote these beautiful words. Perhaps, he wrote the Psalm as a young man when he would sit on a Judean hillside watching over his father's flock of sheep. Perhaps, he wrote the Psalm just before he went out to battle Goliath. Perhaps, he wrote the Psalm later in life, after he had become the King of Israel. Regardless of when it was written, it is a Psalm of faith that leaves no doubt that God is the governing force of all life.

The Twenty-third Psalm is relatively short. The six verses of the Psalm contain only 117 words and is easily memorized. In fact, you could probably repeat the entire Psalm from memory. However, the power of this particular Psalm is not in memorizing the words, but in those words which affirm the never-failing goodness of God. This affirmation is stated so simply as it begins: *"The Lord is my Shepherd . . ."*

As we review this familiar Psalm, I want to look at the promises within which make this Psalm so meaningful in our lives. There are many promises within this Psalm, but there are some specific promises which strengthen us and give us the courage to face whatever comes our way in life.

I. There is the promise of God's care and concern for us. I don't know if you have ever been in areas where the shepherd stays with his sheep. If you have, you have probably noticed that the sheep are very calm and content when the shepherd is present. They know the shepherd is there and that he is interested in them. The shepherd is one who cares for them . . . The shepherd provides them with food and water . . . The shepherd protects them from wild animals in the field . . . The shepherd nurses and cares for them when they are sick . . . They know the shepherd is watching over them and they are calm and content.

The shepherd is one who cares for his sheep because they are valuable to him. From early in the morning until late at night, the shepherd keeps a watchful eye on his sheep because they are important to him.

The promise of this Psalm is that God keeps a watchful eye over us because we are important to him. Yet, one of the deepest tragedies of life is that there are so many people who feel unimportant, worthless, unappreciated, unloved.

Sometimes in just a few weeks I counsel with a half-dozen different people, all struggling with the same issue. They have low self-esteem; they have a low opinion of themselves; they have no sense of their inherent worth or value as people.

Remember a news segment from the presidential campaign of Jesse Jackson. In one segment, they showed him speaking to a high school assembly of teenage boys and girls. He was not talking to them about politics. Instead, he was talking to them about the need for an education and the danger of drugs. He had the auditorium chanting a litany. They were saying:

I am Somebody . . . my mind is a pearl
With it, I can change the world . . . I am Somebody . . .

All of us are born with this need to be somebody. This is a need which seems to be written into our blood. It is a need from which we are never free. It is a need as basic as life — the need to belong and be somebody.

Recently, I was visiting in a local nursing home and noticed an elderly patient shuffling down the hallway very slowly. He wore a frayed bathrobe and he moved as though he had outlived his usefulness. He was confined to that nursing home and had the appearance of one who felt worthless and hopeless.

Then, someone called his name and he stopped and turned toward the sound. The one who called his name was a nurse's aide and she was pushing a cart with crushed ice and water. He leaned against the wall and waited until she caught up with him. When she was standing beside him, a mumbled conversation took place. Disbelief registered on the old man's face, then joy flashed as he smiled. Then he registered a look of determination as he set out to help her in distributing the pitchers of ice. He was needed and he felt important again. The old man still shuffled down the hall, his hands still trembling as he scooped ice into the pitchers . . . and I'm sure that the speed with which the job proceeded dropped drastically. But, there was a look of life about him because he felt useful and needed by someone.

The young nurse's aide began to wonder if he had the strength for his job. She pointed down the hallway and said, "We've got to go all the way to the end of the hall. Can you make it?"

He smiled a toothless smile and said, "Honey, I'd go to the end of the world with you."

We all need to feel like there is a sense of worth or value in our lives. It doesn't matter whether we are rich or poor . . . whether we are young or old . . . whether our name is recognized by everyone or no one. We need to realize that we are someone who is pretty important simply because we belong to the Shepherd of all life. We are important to God and when we recognize his love and care and concern for us, then we will truly know that he is, indeed, our Shepherd.

II. There is the promise of God's understanding. In the Psalm, the shepherd is pictured as knowing and understanding his sheep. He understands that they are afraid of running water because of their heavy wool. Understanding this, the shepherd does not take his sheep to a running river or stream for water. Instead, he searches out and guides his flock to a quiet pool where they can drink.

The shepherd understands that the sheep can be tormented by parasites and insects. Understanding this, he carries a special oil or ointment to rub on their noses and the insides of their ears. This keeps the sheep from being annoyed by the insects and parasites.

The shepherd understands that sheep are always foraging for food. Understanding this, he searches out green pastures where they can have plenty to eat.

The shepherd understands his sheep and tries to meet their needs. The sheep have learned to depend upon the shepherd because he understands them. He is looking out for their welfare. He is interested in them.

It is the same with God. He knows our needs. He knows the problems we face. He knows the fears which leave us trembling like little children. He is our shepherd and he understands everything about us.

I read a story recently about the conductor of the Philadelphia Symphony who was noted for being brilliant. He was also noted for being a stern taskmaster. If any member of the Symphony missed a cue or hit a sour note, he would know and they would face the wrath of the conductor.

In one particular number, a flute solo was featured. It was to be played as if it were coming from a great distance. The conductor instructed the flute soloist to stand off stage where he was to count the measures precisely in order to come in at the exact moment. Since there would be no visual contact between the conductor and soloist, timing was essential. On the night of the symphony, the flute soloist began his solo exactly on cue. The beautiful lilting notes of the flute floated out majestically across that great Music Hall. Suddenly, there was an awful sour note and then complete silence. The soloist did not even finish his piece. The conductor was outraged and at the end of the performance he rushed off stage to find the soloist that ruined the piece.

"Maestro," the player said, "let me tell you what happened."

"There isn't any excuse for your performance tonight," said the conductor.

"Maestro," the flute soloist interrupted, "you know I came in accurately and I was playing beautifully, when suddenly this enormous stage hand ran up, grabbed my flute away from me, pushed me back, and said, 'Shut up, you idiot! Don't you know there's a concert going on out there?' "

The anger drained out of the eyes of the conductor and he said with a smile, "I understand," he said. "All is forgiven."

God is one who understands the problems we encounter. Because he loves us and understands us like a shepherd who watches over his sheep, his forgiveness is always available.

III. There is the promise that God's care never ends. This beautiful Psalm closes out with a mighty crescendo of faith when it declares: *"I dwell in the house of the Lord forever . . ."* Another translation of that verse says: *"I will be in the* presence of God forever . . ." If we have faith in God as the shepherd of our lives, then we can trust that God's care never ends.

In the book, *One Foot In Heaven*, a Methodist minister is at the end of a long and distinguished career. He has a serious heart attack and his son, a reporter with a Chicago newspaper, rushes home to Iowa. When he enters his father's room, the father is very weak, but he is able to smile and say, "Son, if you came for the funeral, I'm happy to disappoint you."

As they sit and talk, the son tells his father about his new promotion. The new job will require him to move from Chicago to New York City. His father smiles and says, "Son, I'm happy about your promotion . . . You will be moving far away. When you return, I probably won't be here . . . But don't worry about me. We are both moving up to new jobs. You know that you are going to New York; and, just as surely, I know where I am going."

When we have faith that the Lord is our Shepherd, we know that God's care never ends. We know that we will dwell in the house of the Lord forever.

The Lord is my shepherd! Is he yours?

What Does God Expect Of You?

Micah 6:8

Ben Powers is the name of a man that may not be familiar to you today. But, several years ago, he made headlines around the world. For the last fourteen years, Ben Powers has worked for NASA. He has been working on the solid rocket motor design and is considered an expert in his field.

In 1987 the ill-fated *Challenger* blasted off for outer space. This was a special mission which included six astronauts and one school teacher, Christa McAuliffe. The astronaunts were to carry out scientific experiments and Christa was to teach some special science classes from the *Challenger* once they were in orbit.

As you know, seventy-three seconds into launch, an O-Ring failed. A startled world watched in shock as the *Challenger* exploded and seven astronauts died, including the young school teacher.

Ben Powers risked the wrath of his supervisors and the scientific community at NASA when he gave his testimony before the Presidential Commission investigating the disaster. Ben Powers was the only NASA engineer who had opposed the launch. He was the only NASA engineer who had expressed concern about a launch in cold weather. He was the only NASA engineer to appear before the Presidential Commission and say that the order to launch had been a bad decision.

Because of his testimony, several key supervisors have been replaced at NASA and Ben Powers is treated like a 'leper' by those with whom he works. He broke the code of silence, and former friends and colleagues now keep their distance.

In an interview, Ben Powers was asked by a reporter if he thought he and his family had paid too high a price for his testimony. Ben Powers was silent for a moment and then he said, "My commitment to Jesus Christ is the most important factor in my life. I did what God expected me to do."

Have you ever asked yourself, "What does God expect of me? How much does God demand of me? How will I know when I am doing what is expected of me?" There are very few verses in the Bible that are better known than Micah 6:8. It is a verse that attempts to answer the question, "What does God expect of You?" Micah asks:

> . . . and what does the Lord require of you but to do justice, and to love kindness, and to walk humbly with thy God?

This particular passage is a profound statement of faith. It is known as one of the four mountainpeaks of spiritual faith in the Old Testament. It presents religion in an easy and understandable style. Micah points out that the only demands which God places on us are to do justice in our daily relationships, to show kindness to other people, and to walk humbly with God.

This may sound like a very easy and simple way to live. But, it is a very costly lifestyle, because its demands are moral and spiritual. It is worth noting that in this statement of faith, two of the parts deal with our relationship to people and one part deals with our relationship to God. This is because it is rather futile to talk about God unless we come to respect the men and women that God created in his image. In 1 John 4:20, the writer says we are not likely to love God whom we have not seen unless we come first to love our fellow humans whom we can see.

As we look at what God expects of us, we are going to be using the three Biblical demands which Micah lifted up.

I. God expects us to do justice in our daily relationships. Justice is such an easy word to say, but it is a difficult word to live because there is so much injustice in our world. We live in a world where there is violence and the innocent suffer. We live in a world where there is hatred and people are hurt. We live in a world where there is hunger and people are starving. We live in a world where there is prejudice and people are denied their basic human freedoms. Doing justice in our everyday lives concerns the passion that you and I must have to see that every person has a decent opportunity to live their lives without fear, and prejudice, and hatred — with the opportunity to live life to its fullest.

Within just a few weeks, our community was recently shocked with two attempts to bring racial hatred out into the open. First, some misguided people by the dark of night vandalized the Jewish Temple and the homes of three Jewish families in our community. They painted Nazi swastikas; they wrote anti-semitic slogans; they tried to intimidate the Jewish families in our community. Then, a week or so later, again by the dark of the night, when cowards gain their courage and seek to hide their own fears, they took the symbol of our faith, the Cross of Jesus Christ, and planted it in the driveway of a black Methodist church. They set the cross on fire to try to intimidate the black people of our community.

But, the people of faith of this community refused to allow the hatred, bigotry, and prejudice of these groups to rule the day. Several hundred people — Christians and Jews, blacks and Whites, Government officials and ordinary people met on a Sunday afternoon in that little black Methodist church.

I was honored and privileged to be one of the speakers. The theme of each speaker was that these acts of prejudice and bigotry do not represent the true feelings of the people of our city.

After the program in that little church, we went outside. Where the cross had been burned in the yard, we planted some trees as a symbol of life. As I was standing and talking to Councilman Goree James, a young woman came up to us. She told us that she was Jewish and her home had been one of three homes vandalized with swastikas and anti-semitic slogans. She said that her two small children were frightened with these attacks on their home and she brought them to this program so they would know that there were others in our community who abhorred bigotry . . . and prejudice . . . and hatred.

She wanted her children to know that others stood for justice for all people. No concept is more Chrisitan or American than this demand for justice. Wherever there are people who are oppressed . . . wherever there are people who suffer discrimination . . . wherever there are people who hate . . . if we are to do what God expects of us, then we must work to bring about justice in our daily relationships. We may not be able to do much about eliminating injustice in the world, but we are expected to bring justice into our daily relationships. Micah phrased it so eloquently when he said:

> . . . and what does the Lord require of you but to do justice . . .?

II. *God expects you to show kindness to others.* Here is the most basic requirement that God expects of us — that we treat other people as we would like to be treated. All good religion begins at this point. But kindness is much more than being harmless. Kindness in the Bible has backbone — it has guts

— it is more than simply being tolerant of others.

One person said, "Kindness isn't really kindness until it costs you something." I don't know if there is a price tag attached to kindness, but I believe that when we go out of our way in being kind to another, we usually bring out the best that is in them.

A school teacher by the name of Miss Thompson found it difficult to like one of her students. His name was Teddy Stallard and he was not interested in school, school work, or anything connected to school. His attitude was so disagreeable that Miss Thompson almost found herself enjoying the Fs she wrote on his papers.

Miss Thompson knew Teddy's background. His school records indicated that in the first grade he had shown some promise. In the second grade, his mother fell seriously ill and Teddy was tabbed a slow learner. In the fourth grade he was far behind and his teacher noted that his father had no interest in Teddy's progress.

Christmas time came and the boys and girls in Miss Thompson's room brought her some gifts. To her surprise, there was a very crudely wrapped present from Teddy. Opening the package, she discovered a gaudy rhinestone bracelet and a bottle of cheap perfume. Sensing that the other children were beginning to smirk and giggle at the gift, Miss Thompson put the bracelet on and opened the perfume. She put some perfume on her wrist and invited the children to smell by saying, "Doesn't the perfume smell lovely?" "Isn't the bracelet beautiful?"

Taking their cue from Miss Thompson's kindness, the children responded with "oohs" and "aahs." At the end of the school day, little Teddy went to Miss Thompson's desk and said: "Miss Thompson . . . Miss Thompson, you smell just like my mother . . . and her bracelet looks real pretty on you, too. I'm glad you like my presents."

From that day forward, Miss Thompson began to show more kindness toward that little boy. And that little boy began to improve — both in grades and attitude.

Many years later, Miss Thompson received a letter from Teddy telling her that he was graduating from high school — second in his class. Four years later, she received another letter from Teddy telling her that he was graduating from college first in his class. And four more years later, there was another letter to inform her that this young fellow who had given her a gaudy bracelet and a bottle of cheap perfume was now Theodore Stallard, M.D. Also, he was getting married and his father was now dead, too. Would Miss Thompson be willing to sit where his mother would sit for the wedding if she were alive? "You're all the family I have left now," wrote Teddy.

Miss Thompson sat proudly where Teddy's mother would have sat for that wedding. That moment of kindness many years before had brought out the best in that young boy.

Kindness may cost you something in time . . . money . . . in pride. But, kindness is what God expects you to show to other people. As Micah phrased it so poignantly:

. . . *and what does the Lord require of you but . . . to love kindness . . .?*

III. God expects you to walk humbly with him. Moffatt, in his translation of the Bible, has translated "to walk humbly with our God" as "to live in quiet fellowship with your God." Living in quiet fellowship with God is simply living one's life and doing the things God would be doing. There are all kinds of opportunities for us to be the living presence of God in our daily lives.

41

Jack Stephens once received a telephone call from a friend who wanted a favor. A problem had come up in his family and he wanted Jack to fill in for him by taking a young boy and his mother to a hospital. The boy had leukemia Jack was told, and probably had only a short time to live. Since the boy's home was only a few blocks away from his own, Jack Stephens agreed to his friend's request.

About thirty minutes later, the mother and the little boy were sitting in the front seat of Jack's car. The child was so weak that he was lying with his head against his mother's shoulder and his feet were stretched out across the seat, resting on Jack's right leg.

After starting the motor, Jack glanced down at the little boy who was staring at him. Their eyes met and Jack smiled at the little boy.

"Mister," the little boy asked, "are you God?"

Jack was surprised by the question. He answered softly, "No, son. Why do you ask?"

The little boy was still staring at Jack as he said, "Mama said that God would come soon and take me away with him."

And Jack realized that at that moment for that little boy in his car, he had been.

So often, people think that "walking humbly" with God means doing a lot of things that appear to be religious, like preaching or becoming a missionary or teaching a Sunday school class. There is nothing wrong with any of these activities. However, "walking humbly with God" simply means living our lives so others can see something of God in us. "Walking humbly with God" simply means living in quiet fellowship with God. "Walking humbly with God" simply means that you seize those opportunities to do the things that God would be doing.

So, what does God expect of you? Micah put it so simply and yet so eloquently when he said:

. . . and what does the Lord require of you but to do justice, and to love love kindness, and to walk humbly with thy God?

Are you doing what God expects of you?

A Season Of Joy

Luke: 2:8-18

One evening I ran into the cleaners to pick up my shirts. They had told me they would be ready, but now they couldn't find them. They began searching and I stood there thinking, "This is great. Every dress shirt I own is at the cleaners — except for the one I'm wearing."

While I was waiting for them to find my shirts, a woman walked in carrying an old laundry basket. Inside the laundry basket, lying on a green towel were five little puppies. They were about five or six weeks old — cute little balls of brown, playful fur.

While we were admiring the puppies, a boy about eight or nine years old walked through the door. He had a big smile on his face as he looked at all of the puppies in that laundry basket. He looked up at the woman and asked, "What kind are they?"

The woman replied, "They are Yorkshire Terriers. They don't get much larger than this."

The boy just kept looking and smiling at those puppies. The woman picked one up and asked him, "Would you like to hold this one?"

A simple look at the boy's face and we knew it was a silly question. Very carefully, he cuddled the puppy in one hand, stroked the puppy's head with his other hand, held the puppy close and softly talked to him.

As I looked around the room, each one of us — the five or six customers and the clerk — was smiling. In that moment, there was joy in our hearts and lives as we watched that little boy cuddle the puppy.

As we move through each Christmas season, we are aware that joy came into this world for more than a moment. Joy came into this world to stay in the birth of the child of Bethlehem. There is no other religion in the world that presents its God as a helpless baby. You want your God to be king . . . You want your God to be large . . . You want your God to be in control of everything. That is the picture we had of God until that night long ago in Bethlehem. On that night, the God of all creation deemed it proper to send his Son to walk among us. A Madison Avenue promoter would undoubtedly have made a big deal of it, with the baby born of a queen and the father a king. But, God is much more resourceful . . . much more sophisticated . . . much more artistic. He had his Son born of a simple peasant girl.

And the place of the Baby's birth wasn't in a big palace. It was in a stable where the cattle and other animals looked on. Everyone loves a baby and there is a certain joy which fills our hearts when we hear of the birth of a baby.

The shepherds were the first to hear of Jesus' birth. They were watching over their flocks in the fields when they were suddenly startled with an angelic chorus singing:

. . . Behold, I bring you good news of great joy, which shall be to all people. For unto you is born this day in the city of David, a Savior who is Christ the Lord . . .

The announcement is made by the angels with joy. And after the shepherds go to the manger and find the child, one emotion that they experienced is recorded: on the way back they glorified and praised God — they experienced joy!

It seems to me that joy is something we need to give ourselves. It is better than happiness, although happiness is important. In fact, I hope that there are many times when you are happy during the year. However, joy is something that abides. Joy is a kind of being. Joy is a quality. You know when you have joy and when you don't. Joy is the sense of security that things are going to be all right in the long run, however painful they might be now, because of who God is. The shepherds went to the manger and found the child. On the way back to their flocks in the field, they were glorifying God, and they had a sense of joy.

As we deal with the idea of joy, there are three things which I think are important if we see this as a Season of Joy.

I. This can be a season of joy when you have a sense of humor. Before joy can ever really be a part of our lives, we need a sense of humor. This does not mean that we must always be laughing. That would be absurd. Some things are so critical that laughter would be inappropriate. But, a sense of humor is a flexible way of being able to enjoy life.

A while back, I heard two women discussing the state of their health. They talked of poor eyesight, hearing problems, and various other ailments. One woman turned to the other and asked, "Do you have a cataract?"

The other woman smiled and said, "No, I have a Buick."

This is a good example of how well a sense of humor enables you to look past the problems of life and experience life with a sense of joy. There are times when a sense of humor can turn tense situations into laughing situations.

Some time ago, I was speaking in a church that had recently redecorated their parlor. In decorating the parlor, the wallpaper they chose had large flowers — black and red and brown and white flowers. When you walked into the room, that flowered wallpaper was the first thing that caught your attention. It was loud, but tastefully done.

When the redecoration was finished, they held an open house, and a visitor walked into the parlor and said, "I don't like it! It's too loud. I wonder what a bride would think when she walked into this room?"

A woman standing beside her, a member of the church, said, "I was on the decoration committee for this parlor."

Without a moment's hesitation, the visitor smiled and said, "They outvoted you, didn't they?"

Now, that is just about as quick as you can be. I am sure that there are times when every one of us would wish to be that quick. A good sense of humor can diffuse a tense situation and enable us to experience life with a sense of joy.

II. *This can be a season of joy when we learn to look within ourselves.* You may see joy in the hearts and lives of others all around you, but the difference comes when you, yourself, begin to experience joy. You can tell me all about friendship and I may see friendship all around me, but there will not be a significant difference for me until I become a friendly person. When friendship gets inside of me, I am changed.

There is a great difference between talking about or observing joy in the lives of others, and being a person whose life is filled with joy. Joy is within you or you don't have it. If it is not within you, as far as you are concerned, it is nowhere. Joy is something you experience in an inward way.

Some time ago, someone asked me, "Robert, if your house caught on fire, what one thing, after your family, would you want to save?"

What would you save from your house? I thought about some expensive items like the televisions . . . or the china . . . . or the silver dinnerware. But, the more I thought about it, I knew what I would save if I could save only one item. I would save the family photo album. It has pictures of my grandparents, my parents, and there are photos of my wife and me on our wedding day. It also has pictures of the children from the day they were born up to the present.

What is that photo album worth? I don't really know. It's probably not worth very much monetarily. If you took it to a flea market, you might get a few dollars, but not much more. But, it is important to me! And do you know why it's important to me? It is important because it contains a pictorial history of my family.

I think you can understand why that family photo album is important to me. It is important for the same reason that so many things are significant to you and me — it's what's inside. It is the people you share life with . . . the memories . . . those moments you treasure. And that is where you find joy in life. It is what the angel was announcing to the shepherds in the field:

> . . . *Behold I bring you good news of great joy which shall be to all people* . . .

You find joy inside your own life. Your life can be filled with joy. That was announced when Jesus was born, and Jesus taught that all of his life.

Are you looking for joy?

Then look within yourself and discover what is truly important. When you do, you will be filled with joy.

III. *This can be a season of joy when we learn to find it in a relationship.* I think we find joy in relationship with people and with God. In Scripture, we are told that a Savior is born. Luke, the physician, phrased it so simply when he wrote:

> . . . *for unto you is born this day in the city of David, a Savior, who is Christ the Lord.*

The birth of this Savior means that God has come to be with us. No matter what we experience in life, whether it is trouble, or sickness, or disappointment, or joy, or happiness, or whatever, the message of the Christmas season is that God, the Heavenly Parent, has come to establish a relationship with us. He loves us even as a human father loves his children . . . even as a mother loves her children.

Several years ago, when I was pastoring the little Methodist Church in Wagoner, Oklahoma, I was invited to teach a session at the United Methodist Women's School of Missions in Oklahoma City. I was to teach in the School of Missions and stay in one of the dorms at O.C.U. I brought my son Jeff along with me, and he was quite small.

That night as we were getting ready for bed, I helped him get into his pajamas, listened to his prayers, kissed him good night, and tucked him into one of the twin beds. Then, I turned off the lights and crawled into my own bed. In the silence, I heard a little voice ask, "Daddy, are you there?"

"Yes, Son, I'm here. You go to sleep."

Everything was quiet for a little bit and then I heard that little voice again, "Daddy, are you there?"

"Yes, Son, I'm here. You go to sleep."

"But, Daddy," said that young, frightened voice, "I'm scared."

"It's okay, Son. I'm here. You just close your eyes and go to sleep."

"Daddy, can we turn on the light?"

"No, Son. I'm here with you. Just close your eyes and go to sleep."

There was a short period of silence and then the small voice asked, "Daddy, can I come get in bed with you?"

"Yes, Son," I responded.

No sooner had I said that than I heard little feet hit the floor and come running to my bed. He crawled under the covers, snuggled against my arm, and in a matter of moments was fast alseep.

Christmas is a Season of Joy because it tells us of a loving God who came into this world because he loves us as a parent loves his children and is always with us. When we snuggle up against his everlasting arms, we have established a relationship which fills our lives with joy.

Decisive Battles With Temptation

Matthew 4:1-11

It happens so often that it seems almost routine in our modern world. We read or listen to certain stories with interest and then make little jokes about how public figures shoot themselves in the foot when they yield to temptation and it becomes public knowledge. In recent years, we have become privy to the temptations which have seduced several public figures.

Not long ago, Gary Hart was the leading candidate in the Democratic Party for the nomination for President of the United States. But, when he took a cruise on a yacht called *The Monkey Business*, with a young woman named Donna Rice, his race for the Presidency was over. He lost his battle with temptation and his hopes and dreams for the future came crashing down around him.

A Methodist minister with a bright future in the church was tempted with sensual pleasure. Apparently, he became involved with another woman and knew that his hopes and dreams could not survive a scandal. So, the reports speculate, he concocted a story about threats on his life and family. Then he attempted to murder his wife, thus eliminating her from the scene. But, his plot failed and his ministry is at an end.

The soap opera saga of Jim Bakker and Jessica Hahn had just about run its course when the news of Jimmy Swaggart burst into the headlines. Jimmy Swaggart was the Baton Rouge television evangelist who sought to destroy Jim Bakker for losing a battle with temptation. He ranted and raved about excising the malignant cancer from the church of those who give in to temptation while, according to the news reports, he had been giving in to temptation for years, meeting prostitutes at various hotels. I guess he discovered that old adage to be true:

"He who lives in glass houses shouldn't throw rocks . . ."

One can only hope that he also learned the advice of Jesus: "Let him who is without sin cast the first stone . . ."

The point I am making is that temptation is a reality in life. Temptation doesn't just come to public figures, but it comes to each of us and it comes in a variety of ways. Sometimes we are tempted sensually . . . sometimes with power . . . sometimes with greed . . . sometimes with prestige . . . sometimes with jealousy. Temptation comes in a variety of packages and there is not a one of us that is immune. We have all fought our battles with the beast called temptation.

Even Jesus fought decisive battles with temptations. The most important and prominent battle that Jesus fought with temptation took place in the wilderness called Jeshimon, which means The Devastation. This is the desert wilderness where Jesus went shortly after his baptism in the Jordan River. He went out into the wilderness to be alone. He went into the wilderness to think about what kind of Messiah he would be and how he would fulfill his task. And, it was while he was in the wilderness that he battled the temptation of how he was going to use the tremendous powers at his disposal.

Three of the Gospel writers tell the story of Jesus' temptations in the wilderness. Since he was alone in the wilderness, Jesus must have told his disciples about the experience. He was sharing with them his own struggles with the three temptations. The first temptation was to turn the stones into bread. This was the temptation to get men and women to follow him because he could give them material possessions. But Jesus knew he could not bribe people into following him. He rejected this temptation by saying, "Man cannot live by bread alone." The second temptation was to stand on the pinnacle of the temple, which was 450 feet high. If he would leap from this and land among the people without being harmed, then the people would follow him. But, Jesus recognized that faith which was founded on magic or the sensational was doomed to failure when the sensational events ceased to be sensational. And so he rejected this temptation by saying, "You shall not tempt the Lord your God." The third temptation was the temptation to compromise with evil in the world. The tempting voice said, "Fall down and worship me and I will give you all the kingdoms of the world." Even as Jesus struggled with this temptation, he became convinced that one can never defeat evil by compromising with evil.

Just as Jesus had his decisive battles with temptation, so do we. There are three things which I think are important in regard to our struggle with temptation.

I. Decisive battles with temptation are always fought within. We must not believe that every battle with temptation is carried out in the open for all to see. In fact, before any yielding to temptation is carried out in the open, the seeds of temptation have worked their way inside our hearts and minds where they have a chance to germinate and grow.

The most decisive battles of history are always fought on the inner battlefield. Even in a war, behind the outer clash of armies is the quiet debate in the councils of the strategists. Behind the lawyer's stirring plea, winning his case in public court, are his unseen decisions in his private thinking. "Court cases," says the legal proverb, "are won in private chambers." Behind a great career in politics that dares to move the world in a new direction, the strategy is planned in a private chamber where the door is shut. It is on the inner battlefield where every one of us must first fight with temptation. God will not force any person to obey him nor will he shield anyone from temptation. And temptations always begin as an inner struggle in our hearts and minds.

The inner struggle with temptation is not imaginary. It is very real. To this day, you can see the ink stain on the wall of Martin Luther's study. Almost 550 years ago, Luther caused that ink stain by throwing his ink jar at the devil as he tempted him in his own innermost thoughts and desires.

Bishop Fulton Sheen was one of the most respected religious figures in this country. When he was approaching eighty years of age, a young seminarian came to see him. After they had exchanged pleasantries, Bishop Sheen looked at this young man and asked, "What can I do for you?"

The young man was hesitant at first; then he said, "Bishop I just don't know if I can take the vow to become a priest."

Bishop Sheen smiled and asked, "What's the problem?"

The young man said, "Bishop, I just don't know if I can take the vow of celibacy and become a priest. I thought seminary would free me from the fantasies and lust which come into my heart and mind. But, now I am close to ordination as a priest in the church and those desires that used to tempt me are still tempting."

Again, Bishop Sheen smiled and said, "Well, I have been a priest for over half a century and I still struggle with the same inner desires. Just remember that there is no sin in being tempted, but in yielding."

We all face the inner struggle with temptation. This is the battleground where every human being is first confronted with temptation — in the innermost thoughts and desires of our hearts and minds. The one thing we need to remember is that there is no sin in being tempted. The sin comes from when we yield to temptation within.

II. Decisive battles with temptation are choices between good and evil. The battle with temptation always begins within our hearts and minds. But, it isn't long before the temptation moves us to making a choice. The Bible knows and emphasizes this hard demand of choosing . . . of choosing between good and evil . . . of choosing between right and wrong. I like that Psalm which clearly shows that we know the difference between good and evil. The writer of the first Psalm said:

> *Blessed is the man who walks not in counsel of the wicked, nor stands in the way of sinners, nor sits in the seat of scoffers . . .*

Each day we encounter temptations which require us to choose between good and evil. There is no once-and-for-all-time choice, because temptations come to us each day and each day we must choose. There is no aspect of life where a sense of control and purpose is more clearly demanded than in a person's moral character. It is here that we must choose what is right and what is wrong as we battle with temptation.

A few years ago, I was in Washington, D.C. to attend some briefings at Congress. One evening I was invited to a dinner party in one of the Congressional office buildings and it wasn't difficult to notice that there was a lot of drinking. There was one man whom I particularly noticed because of his heavy drinking. I noticed him, not just because he was drinking excessively, but because he was wearing the uniform of an airplane pilot.

When he got up to leave, he was so inebriated that two people had to help him out. Just before he went out the door, he turned and said, "Don't worry! I'll be all right tomorrow."

And I thought to myself, "Here is a man so drunk he can't walk, and he is planning on flying a plane tomorrow."

The moral issue here is the irresponsible choice of this man. I am not talking about the moral issue of drinking; I am talking about lives. I am talking about people. I am talking about the battle with temptation that we encounter every day. Each day we are morally confronted with temptation and we must choose between what is right and what is wrong. When we choose that which is right, our inner strength grows. But, when we choose that which is wrong, we find ourselves on the road to moral destruction — because there is a terrible progression about choosing that which is wrong.

Sir Walter Scott once said, "A horse rider can be up to his saddle in mud in no time if he ignores the first sign of soft earth."

When we give in to temptation and choose that which is wrong once, it is easy to do again. It is so easy to be trapped in the terrible progression of making the wrong choices for our lives that we find ourselves on the path to moral bankruptcy.

III. Decisive battles with temptation are not fought alone. This is the message which the Bible affirms over and over again. When the writer of the Gospel of Mark told the story of Jesus' battle with temptation in the wilderness, he wrote: ". . . the angels were helping Him . . ." Jesus was not left to fight his battle with temptation alone and neither are we. We have One with us who never leaves us alone.

There is a young woman whom I know you would not call attractive. She is rather plain looking and consequently never really had a boyfriend during high school. When she got out of high school, she took a job with a large company. She made friends easily and was invited to a lot of parties. Although she had not lived in a cocoon, she was surprised at what went on at those parties — drinking . . . the use of drugs . . . the casual approach to sex.

It was at one of these parties that she met a young man. At first, she couldn't believe that he was interested in her. But, she began seeing him one or two nights a week for about six months. Then, she discovered that she was going to have a child.

When she told him, it was then, for the first time, that he told her he was already married. He said that he would not leave his wife and suggested that she find some way to deal with her problem without bothering him.

She was devastated. She had loved him and he had only used her. She was hurting . . . She was filled with guilt . . . She was ashamed . . . She felt completely alone. Back in her apartment, she buried her head in her hands and sobbed, "Oh God — help me!" Although she heard nothing or saw nothing, she suddenly knew that God was there with her and that she was not alone. His presence seemed to calm her and she found herself praying. She found herself pouring out all of her hurt and shame and guilt and unhappiness — and she realized that he knew everything about her and yet still loved her.

This is the message that the Bible keeps making over and over. We may make the wrong choices when we struggle with the temptations that come our way in life, but God does not abandon us. God does not forsake us. God does not leave us alone.

This is a hope that is real! It is not false. It is not tarnished. It is not cheap or shoddy. It is real! We have One who is with us and will never leave us alone.

Create Your Own Happiness

Matthew 5:3-12

One night I was sitting up late watching the *Tonight Show with Johnny Carson*. A guest on the program that evening was a ninety-four-year-old man. He spoke of the changes that had taken place during his lifetime and he said he was against all of them. He spoke of the garden that he planted every spring. He introduced his seventy-five-year-old girlfriend who drove him to the NBC studio for his appearance on the *Tonight Show*. He was an interesting guest and it was obvious that his remarks were unrehearsed. They simply bubbled up out of his personality that was radiant and happy. It was obvious that the audience loved this old man and they roared with laughter at some of the things he said.

It was apparent that Johnny Carson liked the old man as well. Finally, Johnny looked at the old man and said, "You must have the wonderful secret of happiness to be so happy and full of life even at ninety-four years of age. Can you tell us what makes you so happy?"

"No," the old man replied, "I haven't any great secret. It's just as plain as the nose on your face. When I get up in the morning," he said, "I have two choices. I can choose to be happy or I can choose to be unhappy. What do you think I do? I simply choose to be happy, and that's all there is to it."

I believe that this is what Jesus was saying in that section of the Sermon on the Mount that we call the Beatitudes. He begins each phrase in poetic fashion as he says, "Blessed are the poor in spirit . . . Blessed are those who mourn . . . Blessed are the meek . . . Blessed are those who hunger and thrist for

58

righteousness . . . Blessed are the merciful . . . Blessed are the pure in heart . . . Blessed are the peacemakers . . . Blessed are those who are persecuted for righteousness' sake.

The word "blessed" is literally translated, "how happy." Apparently, Jesus was telling his listeners in these Beatitudes that happiness is not something that is postponed to some future world . . . that happiness is not something that we will receive somewhere in the future . . . but that happiness is something that we can have here and now.

Happiness is missing in the lives of many people because it is an elusive commodity. But, Jesus is saying in this section of the Sermon on the Mount that if you really want to be happy . . . if you want to know what happiness is all about . . . if you want to discover the real secret of happiness . . . then, you have to follow the positive attitudes outlined in the Beatitudes. In other words, if you follow these principles of happiness, you can create your own happiness. I want to suggest some ways that we can create our own happiness.

I. You create your own happiness by refusing to allow problems to overwhelm you. One of the outstanding qualities of Jesus was that he did not attempt to paint a rosy picture of life for those who followed him. He was crystal clear as to what his followers might expect to encounter. He spoke of persecutions . . . He spoke of crosses to be carried . . . He spoke of facing death . . . Jesus was clearly aware that no one can live their lives without encountering problems. Some of the problems will shake the foundation of our souls. Some of the problems will leave us hurting emotionally. Some of the problems we encounter will leave our hearts aching with grief.

You may not be able to do very much about the problems that come your way in life, but you can choose how you are going to respond! That's right! You can allow the problems that come your way in life to overwhelm you . . . to dominate your life . . . to fill you with doom and gloom . . . or, you can learn to face problems head-on and deal with them. Personally, I've found that when you face a problem and chip away at it piece by piece, you can whittle the problem down to size and deal with it effectively.

This was dramatized very clearly last spring when the big sycamore tree in our back yard broke out of its brick planter. The roots were just below the surface and they were threatening to do damage to the house. So, we had to have the tree taken down.

When the tree expert was hired, I thought he would saw through the trunk and let it fall to the ground. But, he didn't do it that way at all. First, he trimmed off the small upper branches. Then, one by one, he sawed through some of the large limbs. Then, he tied a wire to the top of the tree and staked it down out in the direction he wanted the tree to fall. Finally, he sawed through the trunk and the tree safely fell out away from the house and was easily cut up into fire wood.

Explaining what he was doing, the tree expert said, "We always tackle the tree a little bit at a time. That way, it gets simpler and simpler as we go along."

Whenever some problem rears its ugly head in our lives, we have a choice. We can allow it to overwhelm us and drain all of the happiness and joy out of our lives. Or, we can face it . . . We can chip away at it a little at a time . . . We can whittle it down to manageable size. Once we get a problem under control and refuse to allow it to overwhelm us, I believe that we are on our way to creating happiness in our lives.
II. You create your happiness by following Jesus. Now, what is your secret for living a happy life? There are many paths which promise happiness, but the only real path to happiness is to follow Jesus Christ. Of course, you would expect a preacher to say that! But Jesus Christ loves you and me and

when we discover this, we have discovered the secret to happiness.

For some reason, the other day I was remembering the first sermon I prepared for preaching class in seminary. We would prepare a sermon and then preach in the chapel with all of the other students in class evaluating our preaching style. Later, we would go one at a time and watch ourselves on video tape with the professor.

Since I was in an academic setting, I threw in as many impressive sounding theological words as I could work into that sermon. I used phrases like "Heilghischitika," or "the eschatological meaning of the messianic hope," and "the trinitarian history of God in ecclesiology." Now do you know what that all means? I'm not sure I do either! But, at the time I thought I did.

A day or so later, I went to the viewing room with my preaching professor. I waited for him to be properly impressed with my carefully crafted theological sounding sermon. A couple of times, I saw him smile, but he never said a word while the tape was playing.

Finally, when the tape had run its course, he reached up and flipped the switch off . . . He made a couple more notes on his pad, and then he looked at me and asked, "Robert, why did you go into the ministry?"

A little startled by the question, I replied, "I believe God called me into the ministry to preach the Gospel."

"Well, son," this old professor said, "When you get to pastor a church, just go out and tell the people to follow Jesus Christ and forget about sounding theological."

I'm sure I didn't realize it at the time, but it is probably the most important thing I learned in seminary. It's important because when you are challenged to follow Jesus Christ, you are challenged to respond to his love, to open up your

61

life to him. When you do, you will have discovered that he is the secret of happiness and everything else is secondary.

The State Of The Church

Matthew 28:19-20

The day after Christmas we carefully made our way out of town on the ice. We were on our way to South Padre Island for a few days of rest and fun. It is a long drive to South Texas, and we were glad to finally arrive. When we found the leasing agent for the condo we had rented, I went inside to get the key.

When I went inside the office, the woman at the desk was on the phone speaking Spanish to someone. The longer I waited, the more irritated I became. I was tired after the long drive, I wanted to get moved into the condo, and I didn't like waiting on that woman to get off the phone. Then, she turned toward me and smiled. She said:

> I'm sorry to keep you waiting, but we have a small problem — a real small problem. The maid was cleaning one of our condos and when she went into the bedroom, she found a baby lying on the bed in its car seat.

I was no longer irritated, but concerned. I asked, "Is the baby all right?"

"Yes," she said, "the baby's fine. The maid says that the baby is sleeping, but there are no parents around. Evidently, they left the baby on the bed and loaded up their car and drove off forgetting to go back for the baby."

We went ahead and checked into our condo. A little later I dropped by the office and asked, "Have the parents returned for that baby yet?"

The woman smiled and said, "Yes, an embarrassed father came back to get the baby he had left behind."

Just as that young father had forgotten something very important, it seems that something like this has happened to those of us in the church. A casual glance at the inside pages of our church paper reveals that these are uncertain times for the church. Churches everywhere continue to show a dramatic loss in membership. Recently the United Methodist Church lost another 67,000 members in one year. We have closed several hundred churches, while starting only a handful of new churches. Attendance at Sunday school and worship continues to show a decline.

Unfortunately, the United Methodist Church is not the only denomination paralyzed by these dramatic declines. The Episcopal Church has experienced a membership decline of seventeen percent. The Christian Church or Disciples of Christ have dropped by twenty-nine percent. The Presbyterian Church has experienced a twenty-five percent decline. Even the Southern Baptists, who have not shown much of a decline, if any, are having such inner conflict that it may be a sign of trouble for the future.

The response of the church to these problems has been one of uncertainty and confusion. Like the young parents who forgot their baby, we, as a church, have forgotten something very important. We have forgotten what our mission is as the disciples of Jesus Christ in this world. But, the mission of the church and thus our mission as the followers of Jesus Christ is made very clear in the following scripture lesson. Jesus, in this passage known as the Great Commission, said:

Go, then, to all peoples everywhere and make them my disciples: baptize them in the name of the Father, the Son, and the Holy Spirit, and teach them to obey everything I have commanded you . . .

As we look at and examine the state of the church in today's world, I want to suggest some things we must do if we are to once again begin fulfilling the Great Commission.

I. We must develop a devotional life. A young woman came to see me once because she was going through some problems. She said, "I feel all alone. I don't even think God is concerned about me because I feel so empty on the inside."

"Do you pray or read the Bible on a regular basis?" I asked.

She shook her head no and I said, "Perhaps, you are blocking God's presence in your life by never turning to him. You can't expect to feel God's presence in your life as long as you never seek him."

This young woman is not the only one who neglects an important part of the Christian life. I am afraid that there are many of us who have failed to develop a devotional life of prayer and Bible study. One Sunday I was teaching a Sunday school class and I asked how many in that class had a daily devotion of prayer and Bible reading. I suppose that I should not have been surprised, but only one person in that class had any kind of daily communion with God.

There is little wonder that we are having problems as a church when so many of our members are biblically illiterate and not willing to spend ten minutes a day in prayer. Prayer is of the utmost significance to the Christian because prayer is what links us to God. Prayer is an attitude which ties us to God so that his strength flows through us. Prayer is that communion with God which draws us closer to him.

Of course, the amount of time spent in prayer is not the key issue. The important consideration is the relationship you develop with God. This is what prayer is all about. We pray for our needs . . . our family . . . our concerns. And then, we expand our prayers and begin praying for others. When you join the United Methodist Church, you promise to support the church with "your prayers, presence, gifts, and services." The promise to support the church with your prayers means you pray for the people.

Shortly after I moved to my present pastorate, I was calling on a couple who lived across the street in an apartment complex. When I left the apartment of that couple, I was walking back toward the church when I heard an elderly voice call out, "Are you Reverend Allen?"

I stopped and looked around, but didn't see anyone. I thought I was imaging things so I started to walk on toward the church. Again, an elderly voice called out, "Are you Reverend Allen?"

I stopped again and looked around. I saw no one at first. Then, as I looked at one of the windows, I could see an elderly woman sitting at a window. I smiled and said, "Yes, I'm Robert Allen. What can I do for you?"

"Would you mind coming in and talking to me?" she asked. I went to her door, and went in and visited her. She told me her name and said that she had seen me go in the other apartment and had waited and watched for me to come out. As we sat and talked, she told me how many years she had been a member of my new church. She told me she was ninety-four years old. She told me that certain health problems kept her from going to church anymore. Then, she pointed to one of the church papers with my picture on the front. She said, "I recognized you from your picture. I want you to know that I have prayed for you every day since you were appointed to this church."

I was stunned with a sense of humility. She was praying for me. I think I realized in that moment the sheer power there could be for Jesus Christ and his church if every Christian developed a devotional life.

We may have forgotten where the source of our real power lays as a church, but we can recover that power when we develop our own devotional life . . . when we re-establish our relationship to God . . . when we try to live a little closer to him each day.

II. *We must be God's presence in the world.* Some people have tried to blame the problems of the church in today's world on our involvement in social concerns. I think that is erroneous. I believe that the Gospel of Jesus Christ calls us to be involved in the hurts . . . and pains . . . and wrongs of the world. It was St. Augustine who said, "Without God, we cannot, without us, God will not."

For all of our blindness and blundering, we are challenged to go out into the world in the name of Jesus Christ. We are called to do this because even the least and lowest person is sacred to God.

Did you see the report on *60 Minutes* a while back about the French nun who reached retirement age and didn't feel like retiring? So, she got on her knees and prayed that God would send her to the most desperate spot on earth. And he did! Today, the seventy-nine year old Catholic nun serves God in the "City of Garbage." This is the name of a city on the outskirts of Cairo, Egypt. The people who live in this city collect the garbage from the streets of Cario. They not only collect garbage, but they live in the garbage . . . They eat the food found in the garbage . . . They salvage all of their earthly belongings from the garbage as well. The people of the "City of Garbage" are the most despised people in all of Egypt. Into their midst came this retired nun to live among them . . . to teach them and their children a better way to live . . . to establish schools . . . to urge the government to provide health care and better housing. This one nun has made such an impact among the peole of the "City of Garbage" that they call her Sister Emmanuel which means God with us.

When we dare to try and be God's presence in the world, we are living out what it means to be one of his disciples and we are fulfilling his great commission. Are you living your life so that others can see Jesus in your life?

III. We must lead others into the life of faith. While we respect the religious freedom guaranteed by our Constitution to worship God or to completely ignore God, our Christian faith affirms that we all have a common need. We all need a Savior. We all need to experience God's love in Jesus Christ. We all need to respond to Jesus Christ who died on the Cross of Calvary.

If we are to be his disciples in this world, we must lead others into the life of faith. The disciples didn't hesitate when they went out into that heathen world and declared: *"Jesus is the way, the truth, and the life."* We must not hesitate either! We must lead people into the life of faith. This is not only the preacher's task, but it is the responsibility of every Christian. This is the "rent" that all Christians pay; this is the continuing work of everyone who claims a faith in Jesus Christ.

If there is any area in which we have failed, it is in this area of accepting our responsibility to lead others into the life of faith. Once, I was having lunch with a man whom I was attempting to convince to make a commitment to Christ and join our church. When I found out where he worked, I mentioned the name of a member of our church who worked for the same firm. This man sitting across the table opened his eyes wide in amazement and said, "Is he a Christian? I've worked with him for almost ten years and he has never mentioned his faith at all!"

I am not trying to imply that our church member was not sincere in his Christian faith — he simply was not very intentional. He was not seizing those opportunities with his business associates, friends, neighbors, or relatives, to share his faith. He was not actively living out his faith and trying to lead others into the life of faith. If we are to fulfill the Great Commission, then we must pay our "rent" as Christians and cultivate those opportunities to try and lead others into the life of faith and the church. I am not suggesting that we grab others by the arm and ask, "Are you saved?" I am simply suggesting that we need to care enough about people to go out of our way to build a relationship that offers us the opportunity to lead them into the life of faith.

In one of my previous churches, there was a contractor with a wife and two teenage boys. I had invited him numerous times to church and I was getting nowhere. Quite by accident one day, I discovered that he loved baseball. In fact, he was so good at the game that a professional scout had offered him an opportunity with the Cleveland Indians when he was eighteen or nineteen years old.

He was a good ball player, but not quite good enough for professional baseball. One afternoon I stopped by his office and I'm sure he thought I was going to invite him to church again. But, I surprised him by saying, "Ron, I've been thinking about trying to get a church baseball league started. Would you like to help?"

He was surprised by my question for a moment and then he smiled broadly and said, "I'd love to help. What do we need to do?"

We started holding organizational meetings with the other churches in town. We wrote the league rules, established the entry fees, arranged for the use of a field, hired umpires, and made out schedules for league play. One Sunday, I looked up and saw my softball friend and his entire family sitting in church. One Sunday not long afterward, I gave the invitation to Christian discipleship and this man and his family came down the aisle of the church.

As Christians, we are challenged to let others see Jesus Christ in our lives. We must establish relationships . . . we must be a friend . . . we must lead others. A disciple of Jesus Christ is not simply a preacher who stands in the pulpit or a missionary who goes to some foreign land, but a disciple is one who sees the Cross of Jesus Christ and leads others into his saving presence.

Will you be one of his disciples?

I Believe In Prayer

I don't suppose that it comes as any surprise to you that a minister would stand in a pulpit and affirm, "I believe in prayer." You would expect this affirmation. But, belief in prayer came normally and naturally for me as a child. Even before I can remember, I was taught to pray. The first prayer I was taught was the bedtime payer that almost all children learn. It is a simple little prayer which says:

Now I lay me down to sleep;
I pray the Lord my soul to keep.
If I should die before I wake;
I pray the Lord my soul to take.

As I grew older, prayer was simply a natural part of my life. I was firmly convinced that prayer was important . . . that prayer was real . . . that prayer made a difference. And through all the years of my life, I have never had any reason to change that opinion.

When my children were old enough, my wife or I would read them bedtime stories. We read Mother Goose . . . and Aesop's Fables . . . Bible stories . . . and the Great Brain Series. We read the Hardy Boys . . . and Nancy Drew mysteries. Finally, when the story was over for the evening, it was time for our bedtime prayers. We taught our children to pray because we believed in prayer.

I shall never forget the evening we had a special service at church. To close out the service, I simply invited those who

71

desired to come down and kneel at the communion rail for a few moments of prayer. Many, many people got up from their pews and made their way to the front to kneel down and offer up their prayers. As I looked out at those who were kneeling in prayer, I noticed my own children kneeling at the altar. They had not been prodded by their mother and I had not told them to come. They came simply because they believed prayer was important; they came simply because they believed that prayer could make a difference; they came simply because they had some need in their lives that they wanted to talk over with God.

I would guess that today's churches are full of people who believe in prayer. Because they believe in the value of prayer, they fully understand the request of the disciples who asked Jesus one day: *"Lord, teach us to pray."*

As far as the records go, this is the only thing that the disciples explicitly asked Jesus to teach them — how to pray. This seems a little strange because they had prayed all of their lives. However, when they began following Jesus, they saw what prayer meant to him. The Gospel of Luke describes the scene this way:

> *It came to pass, as He was praying in a certain place, that when He ceased, one of His disciples said unto Him, Lord, teach us to pray, even as John also taught his disciples.*

Evidently, they had been observing what prayer meant in his life. He went into prayer in one mood and came out in another. Praying for Jesus was not just a form, but a force, a power. Prayer was vital and influential in his life and they wanted him to tell them how to pray.

Watching Jesus awakened their belief in prayer. As they watched his personality grow stronger, they began to see that prayer was more than just begging God for the things they desired. Apparently, their prayers had been limited to asking God to give them this or give them that. But, now they saw how prayer influenced his life and they asked him to teach them this art of praying.

Today, as we look at the idea of prayer, I want to stress some important points about prayer.

I. Prayer is a powerful force. Prayer is a powerful force that is available to us. Ages ago Isaiah affirmed this as a fact when he said:

They that wait upon the Lord shall renew their strength
. . .

And centuries later we still know that prayer is the most power-ful form of energy that one can generate because prayer is what links us to God.

There are many reasons why people pray. Sometimes we treat prayer almost as if it were magical. We try to manipu-late God to get him to do what we want done.

A mother sent her fifth grade boy up to bed. In a few minutes she went to make sure that he was getting in bed. When she stuck her head into his room, she saw that he was kneel-ing beside his bed in prayer. Pausing to listen to his prayers, she heard her son praying over and over again. "Let it be Tokyo! Please dear God, let it be Tokyo!"

When he finished his prayers, she asked him, "What did you mean, 'Let it be Tokyo'?"

"Oh," the boy said with embarrassment, "we had our ge-ography exam today and I was praying that God would make Tokyo the capital of France."

Prayer is not a magical means by which we get God to do what we want. Prayer is an inner openness to God which allows his divine power to be released in us. Ultimately, the power of prayer is not that we succeed in changing God, but that God succeeds in changing us.

I called for some time on a young man who suffered from Lou Gehrig's Disease, or ALS. I suppose that this is one of the most debilitating illnesses known. Over a period of time, all of the muscles of the body become useless. But, the mind remains clear and sharp — trapped in a body that cannot move.

Of course, this man reacted the way you or I would expect. He was bitter and angry at what was happening to him. When he did pray, his prayers were questions that asked, "Why me, God? Why is this happening to me?"

Once, when I called on him, he cursed me . . . He cursed God . . . He cursed his illness. And who could blame him? He could no longer care for himself. He could no longer sit up without assistance. He required a plastic tube of oxygen attached to his nostrils just to breathe.

After he finished his angry tirade about what had happened to him, he was embarrassed and he apologized. I looked at him and told him, "Don't worry! You didn't shock me or God."

A serious look crossed his face and he said, "I've tried to pray. I've asked God to cure me, but I keep getting worse."

"Perhaps," I said, "you are praying the wrong prayer. The promise of God is not that he will magically remove our problems but that he will give us strength in the midst of our problems. Why don't you start praying for strength to deal with your illness and strength to enjoy the life you have?"

I would be lying if I said the change was immediate. But, gradually a change took place. The bitterness and anger he felt gave way to acceptance. But, the surprise was that he saw an avenue of ministry. With a pencil between his teeth, he began typing out notes to people who were going through problems. They were not long, just short, simple notes telling others that someone was thinking about them and praying for them. Shortly before his illness claimed his life, he told one of the members of his family, "I have enjoyed my life to the end."

Prayer is a powerful force. The power of prayer is not in changing God, but in changing us from unhappy individuals to happy ones, in changing bad men and women to good men and women, in changing the cruel into the kind. If we make a place for prayer in our lives, we will be amazed at the power and strength which is released in our lives.

II. Prayer brings comfort. I like the old story of a minister who went camping up in the mountains. He was enjoying the hiking through the mountain trails until the day he found himself face to face with the biggest . . . ugliest . . . meanest . . . grizzly bear he had ever seen. He saw no means of escape and the bear was coming toward him growling. The minister did the only thing he knew to do. He dropped to his knees, closed his eyes, and began to pray. The longer he prayed, the better he felt. The bear had not attacked. So, the minister opened his eyes to see where the bear was and the bear was kneeling right in front of him. The minister was overjoyed and said, "O, Brother Bear, this is wonderful. It is a comfort to my soul to know that we are praying to the same Lord."

The bear opened his eyes, looked at the preacher, and said, "Brother, your comfort is going to be short-lived because I'm saying grace."

There are many different reasons to pray, but one of the most valid reasons is to find comfort and peace. George Buttrick said, "prayer is as elemental as a cry in the dark." When we cry out in the dark, we are searching for some comfort . . .

some peace . . . some hope . . . in the midst of the problems of life. Real prayer is calling out to God in the midst of the pain and hurt — looking for some comfort.

In ordinary life, we run into those occasions when we are up against something which is too much for us, or we undertake something which is too hard for us. It is moments like this when we cry out in the darkness. It is moments like this when we lift our hearts and souls to God hoping to discover some comfort and peace — And our hope is not disappointed! "God is our refuge and strength in a time of trouble." When we pray to God in a time of need, we discover his strength and his comfort and his peace.

I know a woman who was left a widow at a rather young age. She was not only grieving at the loss of the man she loved; she was also grieving at the responsibility of raising two small girls alone. She was frightened for herself and she was afraid she would have to give the children up.

One day, the despair was so overwhelming that she walked three blocks to the Methodist Church. The door was unlocked and she slipped inside and sat in the back pew. As the sunlight streamed through the stained glass windows, she cried out her fears to God. "How was she to raise two girls alone?" There were no day care centers in those days and she wondered what would become of the girls if she took a job?

As she sat in that church that day, she heard no voice from the heavens. But, for some reason, her fears were relieved. And as she sat there, an idea began to take shape in her mind. She would support her family by giving piano lessons in her home.

So, by giving piano lessons to as many as eighty children a week (two of them were my children), and by carefully managing her money, she raised her two children and sent them to college. She died a couple of years ago at ninety-four years of age. About thirty minutes after her last piano lesson of the day, a sudden heart attack claimed her life.

She was an ordinary lady, who made an extra-ordinary discovery. She discovered a comfort, she discovered a peace, she discovered a strength, when she cried out to God from the darkness of her soul.

III. Prayer affirms that we are not alone. Prayer affirms the fact that even when we are alone, we are not alone. This is one of the most profound and mysterious facts in human life — the consciousness that being alone, we are not alone. We may see in the Garden of Gethsemane a picture of a universal human experience. Jesus left the world outside the garden gate. Jesus left the major group of his disciples at the Garden gate. Jesus left his three closest friends within the Garden gate. And then in solitude he went out under the olive trees. But, there, alone, he was not alone.

Explain that experience as we will, it cannot be explained away. Elijah, amid the loneliness of the desert, heard the still small voice. Even when we are alone, we are not alone. This is a fact of human experience which cannot be explained away.

I believe in prayer because it affirms that no matter how lonely we are, there is still one to whom we can turn. God is that One who does not leave us alone.

Do you remember the old story in the book of Daniel about the three Israelites cast into the fiery furnace? According to the story, they walked through the fiery furnace without being burned. They walked through the fiery furnace without their clothes being singed. They walked through the fiery furnace with One who was like unto the Son of God.

Who of us here does not need that experience? There is no fiery furnace so hot that there is not One who walks with us . . . One who does not leave us alone . . . One who is a divine companion, from everlasting to everlasting, a God who loves you and me!

77

I Believe In Heaven

John 14:2; Luke 23:39-43;
1 Corthinans 2:9

In 1816, Lord Byron wrote a narrative poem that has become a classic. The poem is entitled, "The Prisoner of Chillon," and it is the story of a man incarcerated in the dungeon at the Castle of Chillon near Lake Geneva, Switzerland.

The prisoner was in a narrow, cramped dungeon cell for such a long time that he began to think of it as home. He made friends with the spiders, insects, and mice that shared his cell. They were all inmates of the same dungeon and he was monarch of each race.

The years in the dark dungeon cell had taken their toll. He was no longer unhappy or uncomfortable. He had grown accustomed to his environment and came to think of his chains as friends.

One day a bird perched on the crevice of the ledge above and began to sing. It was the sweetest music he had ever heard. Suddenly, the desire to see the outside world overwhelmed him. He grabbed the walls of his cell, and began climbing and struggling up the wall so that he could look out of the little window. In that moment, he saw a world that he had forgotten. There was a crystal blue lake . . . and some tall green trees . . . and the beautiful little white cottage that he called home nestled against the green hills . . . and an eagle soaring majestically across a blue sky.

He saw them all for one magnificent moment and then he fell back into his cell. But that dungeon cell was no longer home. For one fleeting moment he had seen a home that lay beyond the tiny cramped cell of the dungeon. He had seen a vision of a world beyond and hope eternal towered over the despair.

We, too, have a vision beyond our present existence. We are pilgrims of the future because our faith enables us to catch a glimpse of an everlasting Kingdom which lies beyond this world. Jesus said:

In my Father's house are many mansions: if it were not so, I would have told you. I go to prepare a place for you . . .

The Apostle Paul spoke of the fantastic hope that each of us has beyond this world when he said:

The eye has not seen, nor the ear heard, neither have entered into the heart of man, the things which God has prepared for them that love him . . .

Jesus affirmed this hope of an eternal Kingdom beyond this existence as he was being crucified on the Cross. One of the men being crucified with Jesus turned to Him and asked: *"Jesus, remember me when You come into Your kingdom . . ."*

No one else in the Scripture ever called him Jesus. They called him Master . . . They called him Jesus of Nazareth . . . They called him Jesus, son of David . . . They called him teacher or Rabbi . . . They called him the Christ. But no one else called him Jesus!

In an hour of need, this criminal hanging on a cross saw some hope in Jesus and requested: *"Jesus, remember me when You come into Your kingdom . . ."* What comfort it must have been when Jesus turned toward the dying thief and said: *"Today, you will be with me in Paradise . . ."*

The promise of Jesus is that there is something which lies beyond this life. God does not create life and allow it to end in a moldy six-foot hole in the ground. The promise of Jesus has become our eternal hope. As plainly as I know how, I am affirming that I believe in this hope. I believe with all of my heart and soul in the Christian doctrine of eternal life. I believe in heaven.

Today, as we look at this idea or concept of heaven, I don't want to draw you a blueprint of heaven. In fact, there is no way that I could prove the idea of heaven. I don't believe it can be proven scientifically. I don't believe the idea of heaven can be proven theologically. I don't believe the idea of heaven can be proven philosophically. So, instead of trying to prove "beyond a reasonable doubt" the idea of heaven, I simply want to affirm what I have come to believe over the years.

I. I believe that in heaven there will be continued growth. So often we think of our imagery of heaven as fact. The Bible uses a lot of beautiful poetry to describe heaven. It speaks of pearly gates. It speaks of Gabriel blowing his trumpet. It speaks of angels' wings. It speaks of singing and praising God all day long.

These are our pictures; this is our imagery. But, if this is all there is to heaven, I believe that we would become bored after a short time. After all, singing hymns for eternity would be three or four songs more than I want to sing.

There is an old story about a man who complained that he had too much work to do. He never seemed to be caught up. Every day for twenty years he looked at his desk piled high with unfinished projects . . . letters to be answered . . . bills to be paid . . . and problems to be solved. When he walked out of the house to get away from the clutter, he saw the grass that needed to be cut and the hedges that needed to be trimmed. If he could only get caught up, just once, he thought that would be heaven.

One night he dreamed that he was in a large room with a beautiful mahogany desk before him. The desk was clean . . . and bright . . . and shiny. There were no letters or bills or problems waiting to be solved. Through the window he could see the lawn freshly mowed and the hedges meticulously manicured. It was a great relief. He had caught up at last and now he could enjoy some peace and quiet.

But, now he had nothing to do — nothing but to sit and stare out the window. As he was staring out the window, he noticed a postman walking down the street — but there were no letters in his bag. He called out to the postman and said, "I see you don't have anything to do either?"

"Nope," the postman said, "not a thing."

"I don't know," the man said, "if I like a heaven where there's nothing to do."

"Don't you know?" the postman asked. "This isn't heaven, my friend, this is hell!"

There was nothing to do and it was hell to him. And I believe that a heaven where there is nothing to do but sing hymns . . . and walk the streets of gold . . . and flutter around with angels' wings . . . would be a heaven that is not very appealing. Personally, I like the concept of a heaven where there is continual growth.

Winston Churchill, in his book, *Painting As A Pastime*, said:

> *When I get to heaven I mean to spend a considerable portion of my first million years in painting, and so get to the bottom of the subject . . .*

I believe in a heaven that will not be boring, but an adventure; I believe in a heaven where we can continue to grow and develop.

II. I believe that in heaven there will be a time of reunion. When I think of eternal life, I think of the words that Jesus said to the thief on the cross. He said: *"Today, you will be with me in paradise."* Notice those pronouns: you . . . me. Jesus seemed to be saying that they would be together and would know each other.

I sat one night in the home of a family who were grieving. Their nineteen-year-old daughter had skidded on some ice and veered into the path of a semi. The driver of the truck had tried to swerve, but it was too late. He slammed into that girl's car and we were tragically confronted with how thin the thread is that separates us from life and death.

As we sat and talked, the mother held a gold-framed picture of her daughter. And the father looked at me and asked, "Do you really believe that I'll ever see her again?"

He didn't ask if heaven's streets were really paved with gold, and he didn't care if the gates were really made of pearl. He wanted to know if he would see his daughter again.

This is a question that everyone who experiences sorrow wants to know. They want to know if they are going to see their loved ones again. They want to know if they will be reunited with those who go before them.

I don't know if I can adequately explain it, but I believe that our personal identities will survive the deaths of our bodies. I don't believe that we will be simply absorbed back into some sort of creative gob. I believe in a concept of heaven where you will still be you and I will still be me. One of the old gospel songs promises:

> *We shall come with joy and gladness,*
> *We shall gather round the throne,*
> *Face to face with those who love us,*
> *We shall know as we are known.*

I believe in a heaven where we will be reunited with our loved ones. My finite mind may not be able to comprehend that which is eternal, but I know that heaven in all its glory would be a disappointing place if we could not see those we love and have fellowship with them again.

III. I believe in a heaven that is an eternal home. I don't believe that heaven is a place on a map that we can drive to. I don't believe that heaven is a place that we can chart on some celestial graph and locate by looking through a powerful telescope. I don't believe that we could locate heaven by traveling to the outermost edges of the galaxy. I simply believe that heaven is our eternal home. This is the way Jesus described heaven in John 14. He said: *"In my Father's house . . ."* I don't think we really need to go much beyond this description of heaven. Heaven is being with God in his house. Heaven is going home to God. Heaven is "dwelling in the house of the Lord forever."

I like the story of the old country parson who spent fifty years in one village church. He served God and the community faithfully. He was not only their pastor, but he was their friend and inspiration in Christian living.

The roads were never so bad that he would not go out and sit and pray with one who was journeying through the valley of the shadow of death. The nights were never too cold to keep him from going to some God-forsaken saloon to help a drunken husband home to his wife and children.

He was the one they sought out in time of trouble. He was the one they called on to perform their marriages. He was the one they wanted to baptize their children. He was the one who comforted them when they had to bury a loved one. He was their pastor and they loved him as much as he loved them.

One Sunday morning when it was time for church to begin, he was not there. As he had grown older, he sometimes slept late. But he had never been this late before. Finally, Andrew, the town blacksmith, went next door to the parsonage to remind him that it was time for church.

He knocked on the door, but there was no answer. He pushed the door open and he found the old pastor slumped over his roll-top desk with his head resting on his open Bible.

Andrew walked back to the church and down the aisle to the front of the congregation. He took off his hat and with tears glistening as they rolled down his cheeks, he said, "We won't be having church services today."

"Why not?" someone asked. "Where's the pastor?"

"He's gone, " Andrew said softly. "He's gone home."

There never was a funeral like the one they had for this country parson. People from all over the county came to pay their respects and to lay a flower upon his grave.

On his tombstone, they simply engraved the words of the blacksmith, "He's gone home."

Yes, I believe in heaven! 1. I believe in a heaven of continued growth. 2. I believe in a heaven where we will be reunited with our loved ones. 3. I believe in a heaven that is our eternal home.

You can claim this heaven as your own when you give your heart and life to Jesus Christ.

I Believe In Judgment

Matthew 25:31-33

Recently, I heard a preacher on television preach a sermon on divine judgment. I have no doubt that he is sincere in his beliefs. He is very good at using words and manipulating the emotions of his audience. He is charming, witty, and entertaining. But his interpretation of judgment degrades God from a Heavenly Father to a heartless tyrant.

He drew a picture of God which makes my heart shudder, because his idea of judgment is punishment. He believes that sinners will be cast into utter darkness. He believes that sinners will be thrown into an eternal lake of fire; He believes they will burn in the fires of hell forever. He quoted a little poem about burning in hell forever. The poem said:

> "Forever" is written on their racks,
> "Forever" on their chains;
> "Forever" burneth in the fire,
> "Forever" ever reigns.

I have trouble with this interpretation of judgment because God is better than that. I realize that the Bible quotes Jesus very clearly about Hell being a "lake of fire." But, I also think it is important to understand that Jesus used word pictures to describe many abstract concepts. Once he pointed to the birds of the air and said that not one of them falls to the ground without the Heavenly Father knowing. Once he pointed to flowers growing in the field and said that Solomon in all his glory was not arrayed as one of these. Once he said that even the hairs of our head were numbered. Jesus often used word pictures to describe abstractions about God which he never intended to be taken as physically literal.

When Jesus spoke of hell, he was using a word picture. The Greek word for hell is *Gehenna*. In the Hebrew it is *Hinnom*. Literally, hell was the Valley of Hinnom or the Valley of Gehenna and it lay on the outskirts of Jerusalem.

It was in this valley where in the ancient days those who worshipped the heathen god, Moloch, had sacrificed Jewish children. To the Jews, this valley became desecrated territory and to show their utter contempt of the heathen god, Moloch, they turned this valley into the garbage dump for Jerusalem. It smoldered continuously with fires. In it a loathsome species of worms bred and multiplied. The bodies of the worst criminals were thrown into this valley. In fact, the worst fate that could come to any Jew was to not have a place to be buried, but to be thrown into the fires in the Valley of Gehenna, or Hinnom. Therefore, it was natural for Jesus to use hell or Gehenna as a word picture of God's judgment on those who were rebellious against his love. Hell, with its flames and eternal torture, was not meant to be taken physically and literally.

However, I must affirm to you very simply that God's judgment is a reality. It is not a pleasant thought, but God is a God of judgment. For centuries we have asserted this belief in the Apostles' Creed when we say: "He shall come to judge the quick and the dead . . ."

Anne of Austria once said, ". . . God does not pay at the end of every week, but at the end He pays."

We can go on with our lives and leaving God out, disobeying his laws, and failing to be the people he calls us to be. But, we need to remember that judgment is a reality. The most definite evidence of its reality is Jesus' parable on the last judgment. At the end of the parable, the sheep are separated from the goats with unerring certainty.

With this same certainty, I believe that there will be judgment in our lives. We cannot get away from it because it is a reality. I want to look at the idea of judgment. I am not going to look at judgment from the perspective of a fiendish God who is seeking to punish us. Instead, I want to look at the judgment of God from the perspective of the life of Jesus who taught us that God is loving . . . God is forgiving . . . God is compassionate . . . God is interested in each of us. I want to look at three ideas which I believe are important in dealing with the idea of judgment.

I. I believe judgment is happening every day. Every day is judgment day. Every life is being shaped by the small events of everyday life. There is no way to get around this and you are becoming what you do and say every day. Eternity does not start when we die; it is here now. We are in eternity right now and we don't have to be afraid of it. The same God we are going to be with forever is the God we are with now, and we are judged every day of our lives.

I heard about a man in court, standing before a judge. The man said to the judge, "God being my judge, I am not guilty."

And the judge replied, "God is not your judge today; I am and you are."

This is how we are. We are guilty and we are judged every day of our lives. We are judged daily on the basis of our actions.

A friend invited me to lunch once. I am sure that he didn't invite me out simply for lunch. He wanted to show off his new sports car. He had a black Porsche and he was very proud of that new car. He was so proud of it, that he tried to protect it on his office parking lot. He was afraid someone would open their car door and bang it against his while it was parked.

So, he started parking in such a way that his car took up two spaces. That way, no one could park close enough to bang their car doors into his new sports car.

The only problem with this was that when the lot filled up, someone was denied a parking space. One day this man came out to his car and found a note on his windshield which said: "You lucky devil, you! You found two parking spaces and I couldn't even find one."

He was judged on the spot and found guilty. It didn't take him weeks or months to realize that what he was doing was wrong. Someone, in a very polite way, judged him guilty that very day.

We need to realize that we are judged regularly . . . We are judged daily . . . We are judged everyday of our lives. We don't have to wait for some Judgment Day in the future, because every day is a Judgment Day.

II. I believe God's judgment will be tempered with his respect for life. It was God who created us and gave us the ability to make our own decisions. Some of our decisions are right and some are wrong. God is not going to condemn us simply because we make some decisions that are wrong, simply because we come up short of everything he expects of us, simply because we failed to be all that we are called to be.

A few weeks ago, I saw Gregory Peck on the Johnny Carson show. They were talking about the various movies he had made — close to 100 over the years. As they were talking, Johhny asked, "Greg, what do you think was your best movie?"

Without a moment's hesitation, Gregory Peck said, *To Kill A Mockingbird.*

If you have seen that movie, which is based on Harper Lee's novel, you know it is a powerful story. A young black man named Tom Robinson is accused of raping a white girl in Maycomb County, Alabama. It is obvious throughout the story that Tom is innocent. And, it is crystal clear that the racial tensions in this small county in Alabama means that Tom Robinson will be found guilty in spite of his innocence.

However, one white attorney, a man named Atticus Finch, agrees to defend Tom. In spite of the personal threats against his life and the racial hatred expressed by many whites, Atticus Finch puts together a case which proves this white girl is lying about being raped by Tom Robinson.

Throughout the long trial, the blacks of the community gather in the balcony of the courthouse to watch Atticus Finch plead the case and do everything he can to set an innocent man free. But, when the all-white jury brings in its verdict, Tom Robinson is found guilty and sentenced to die.

Tom is led away in chains and the white audience and judge and jury leave the courtroom. The only ones left are Atticus Finch, putting his files in his briefcase, and the blacks in the balcony. Sitting with the black preacher are Atticus' two small children, Jim and Scout. They have sneaked into the courtroom.

Finally, Atticus Finch is ready to leave the courtroom. As he pushes open the swinging gate, every person in the balcony quietly stands — except for his youngest child. The old black preacher leans over and says, "Stand up, Scout. Your father's passin'."

Atticus Finch had failed! Atticus Finch had come up short in his efforts to win the freedom of an innocent man. But, every person in that balcony had a deep respect for Atticus Finch.

And this is the way it is with our lives. Some of the decisions that we make in life are wrong, some of the decisions that we make in life are sinful, and sometimes we come up short in being all that God calls us to be. But, God is going to temper his judgment upon us because of his deep respect for our lives.

III. I believe judgment will be tempered with God's grace. Last, but not least, I want to make this point: God's judgment on our lives will be tempered with his grace. We are saved by God's grace first . . . and last . . . and always. We are not saved by our goodness and we are not saved by the depth of our faith. You and I are saved by grace, and God's grace tempers the judgment we deserve in our lives.

I want to share this story. It is an old story of a man who was met at the pearly gates by the angel Gabriel. Gabriel told the man that entry into heavens required 1000 points. The good works he performed during his life would count toward the points necessary to gain admission to heaven.

The man said, "Well, I was active in my church and attended almost every Sunday."

"That is worth fifty points, " Gabriel said.

The man smiled and said, "I sang in the choir."

"That's good for another twenty-five points," said Gabriel.

The man realized that he only had seventy-five points and needed 1000 if he was going to get into heaven. "Well," the man said, "I taught a Sunday school class of children for three months. How many points is that worth?"

"You get another twenty-five points, " Gabriel replied.

The man was quickly becoming frantic and it didn't look like he would earn enough points. Finally, in frustration, he said, "The only way I'm going to get into heaven is by the grace of God."

Gabriel smiled broadly and said, "Yes, and God's grace is worth 1000 points! Welcome to heaven."

You don't earn your salvation by your good works . . . or by your faith . . . or by your beliefs. You are saved by God's grace! I don't want you to misunderstand. Grace does not whitewash the sins of your lives. Grace comes in a very honest way and says to you: "You made a mistake, you blew it, you made a fool of yourself, you are a sinner, you deserve the judgment of God upon your life." But, the Good News of the

Gospel is that God tempers his judgment with his grace. You are saved by God's grace. This is the nature of God. He loves you. He forgives you. He redeems you. He tempers his judgment upon your life with his grace because of who he is and because of who you are.

I believe the Apostle Paul captured this idea when he wrote:

> . . . *there is nothing in all of creation that will ever be able to separate us from the love of God which is ours through Christ Jesus our Lord* . . .

God tempers his judgment on our lives because of his grace in Jesus Christ.

Isn't it about time you responded to God's love in Jesus Christ?

The Gospel In Miniature

It was in the springtime and I was speaking at a church in a small town in southeastern Oklahoma. We had a large crowd of people in that small church when the thunder began to roll in the distance. Once the service was over, there was a reception in the fellowship hall.

It was one of those occasions when I was in a hurry to get my car and start home before the thunderstorm dropped its rivers of water. However, since the reception was in my honor, I could not slip out early.

After a short while, the claps of thunder were no longer in the distance. They seemed like they were right over the church, because that little church seemed to rattle and quiver with each thunder roll. One look out the door and we knew that no one was going home in that downpour.

While we were waiting, a woman about seventy-five years old came up to me and asked if I had ever seen a miniature Bible. Not really understanding what she meant when she spoke of the miniature Bible, I asked if she had one. She reached into her purse and pulled out a small Bible. It was only about one inch in size and the cover said, "The Miniature Gospel." Opening up the Bible, I saw that the print was so small that it could not be read without a magnifying glass. This lady must have been a Girl Scout, because she was prepared. She handed me a magnifying glass and I was able to make out the words in the Gospels of Matthew, Mark, and Luke which were printed on those small pages. I had to agree with that woman, it was the smallest Bible I had ever seen. It was indeed, a miniature Bible.

However, if you want to condense the Bible, it could probably be distilled to that one verse in John 3:16. In the whole Bible, there is not another verse which has so concisely outlined God's relationship with all of humanity.

Everybody has their favorite Scripture passages, yet this passage has been called "Everybody's text." This one verse contains the very essence of the Gospel. Martin Luther, the great Protestant reformer, called this particular verse, "The Gospel In Miniature."

This is a verse which rings with clarity as it so simply outlines the main themes of the Bible. This is one verse which we all ought to know, which we all ought to memorize, which should be treasured in all our hearts:

For God so loved the world, that He gave His only begotten Son, that whosoever believeth in him should not perish, but have everlasting life.

I can understand why Luther called it "The Gospel In Miniature." It may not tell us everything that is contained within the pages of the Bible, but it does lift up the great themes of the Bible. I want us to look at these themes which are so clearly presented in this beloved passage.

I. The first theme presented is the love of God. I have never been able to understand or agree with those preachers who continually dwell on the wrath of God. They seem to take some kind of sadistic delight in proclaiming the wrath and punishment of God when the whole message of the Bible is condensed into the first six words of John 3:16: "For God so loved the world . . ."

This is the key to understanding God — the fact that he loves. He loves more than one nation. He loves more than one group of people. He loves more than those who love him. He loves the world — all the people of the world. He loves the unlovable and the unlovely. He loves the lonely who have no one else to love them. He loves the man who loves God and the man who never thinks of God. He loves the woman who rests in the love of God and he loves the woman who rejects the love of God. All are encompassed in his vast inclusive love. It was Augustine, one of the great patron saints of the early church who said, "God loves each one of us as if there was only one of us to love."

It is easy to think of God as looking at us and waiting for us to make a mistake. It is easy for us to believe that God is some kind of vengeful God who is going to punish us when we step out of line. But the tremendous thing about this Gospel in miniature is that it affirms that God loves us simply because we are his children.

More years ago than I like to remember, I volunteered to deliver the morning paper for a friend of mine. He was going to be gone during the Christmas recess from school and he needed someone to take care of his paper route.

I realize that Benjamin Franklin thought everyone should be an early riser, but getting up at 4:30 a.m. is almost an impossible task for me. Sometimes, the alarm would go off in my ear and I would almost sleep through its buzzing.

One morning during the Christmas holidays, a blue northerner moved through. The wind was blowing and there was a cold drizzle. Do you know how cold and wet and miserable one can get riding on a bicycle? Even though I was bundled up with extra layers of clothes, I can still remember being so cold that my teeth were chattering.

Once I got the papers folded and loaded on my bicycle, my father pulled up in our '57 Chevrolet. He said, "Son, it is too cold and wet for you to ride your bicycle on the route this morning. Put the papers in the car and I will drive you."

I can still remember that morning, as if it were yesterday. My father had to go to his job. It certainly wasn't his responsibility to see that another boy's paper route was taken care of that day. Yet, he was there because he loved me.

Somehow, when I am trying to define what the love of God means for each person in this world, I think of that cold morning when my father and I threw newspapers from a '57 Chevrolet. He didn't have to be there, but he was because I was his child and he loved me.

God's judgment upon us is not punishment . . . and wrath . . . and destruction. God's judgment upon us is love. We are loved because we are his children. All of us are his children, like the little song says,

Red and yellow, black and white, they are precious in His sight.

God loves each of us because we are his children and we are precious in his sight.

II. *The second theme presented is the gift of God.* Sometimes, as Christians, we act as though God's presence in this world all began with the Christmas event. God has always been in the world, and God has always been the same, but we didn't know it or understand it until he presented us with his gift at Bethlehem. Electricity has been in existence since the creation of the world, but we didn't know it or comprehend it until someone harnessed it. So it is with God! God has always been precisely as he is. The fact that Jesus came into this world and lived among us is God's gift to us.

God's gift is his presence in this world through Jesus Christ. Emmanuel is God's gift in a nutshell. Emmanuel is Hebrew for "God with us." In the first chapter of the Gospel of John, there is a phrase which says:

"The World became flesh and dwelt among us, full of grace and truth."

God's gift is that we are not alone — he is with us because of Christ.

There was a story in the paper some time ago about an elderly man who was dying in a hospital. He had no relatives or family in the community. However, he kept asking for his son and some people at the hospital did some checking and discovered that he had a son who was a Marine in boot camp in South Carolina.

Word was sent to the boot camp and a young Marine made a lonely pilgrimage to the hospital where the old man lay. A nurse took the Marine to the dying man's room. The young man sat down beside the bed and took the old man's shriveled hand. Not a single word passed between them. Finally, just before dawn, the old man quietly slipped through the valley of the shadow of death.

At the nurses' station, when it was all over, the Marine asked, "Who was that old man?"

Startled, the nurse looked up and asked, "Wasn't he your father?"

"No, he wasn't," said the Marine. "I never saw him before last night."

"If he wasn't your father," asked the nurse, "why did you stay?"

"Well," the young Marine said, "When I walked into the room, I knew there had been a mistake and the wrong Marine had been dispatched. But, I also knew that he was dying and needed his son, so I stayed."

We all need someone. Everybody needs someone and God's gift to this world is his presence in Jesus Christ.

Elizabeth Barrett Browning once wrote a love sonnet to her husband, Robert. One morning at breakfast she slipped it into his pocket and ran upstairs. He opened it and read:

The face of all the world
has changed for me,
Since first I heard
the footsteps of thy soul.

This is what the Incarnation means! Footsteps on the shore of Galilee and we know that we are not alone. We know that God's presence is with us through Jesus Christ.

III. The third theme presented is the promise of God. The promise of God is contained in that one phrase which closed out that verse like a mighty crescendo, *"that whosoever believeth in him should not perish but have everlasting life."* That is quite a promise — everlasting life.

Too often we think of eternal life as something that is confered upon us when we are dead and buried and pushing up daisies. But eternal life is something we have right now and it continues through the experience we call death. We are on the road to eternal life if we dare to walk with God today. I love that phrase by the Apostle Paul in Romans 14:8 where he says, *"Whether we live or whether we die, we are the Lord's."* That is a beautiful passage which affirms God's promise to us.

Not too long, one of the funeral homes phoned to tell me that a woman died who was not a member of a local church. She had been listening to our worship services every Sunday on television and her husband and family wanted to know if I could conduct the service.

I checked my calendar and saw that I did not have any appointments, so I said that I would be happy to conduct the service. I asked the family about a convenient time to meet with them and they offered to come by the church. About ten members of the family came by and one of the secretaries put them in the church parlor, then buzzed me to let me know they were there.

The husband told me they had been married for forty-seven years when his wife had a heart attack and was gone. Of course, he was heart-broken at her sudden death and he wanted to know if God could love her even though she never joined a church.

I took his hand and said, "Our God is a loving God. I can't believe that he would create a life and then allow it to be destroyed. I believe that God can be trusted to care for her life. Remember, Jesus said not even a sparrow falls to the ground without God's notice. The promise of God is everlasting life, and I believe that we can trust his promise."

This is the Christian faith! This is the Gospel in miniature!

For God so loved the world, that whosoever believeth in Him, should not perish, but have everlasting life.

Religion In A Nutshell

Mark 12:28-34

Mildred was a fine lady. She was sixty-four years old when the doctors discovered that she had terminal cancer. She was in and out of the hospital several times receiving her treatments, and each time she seemed to be a little weaker than the time before.

Mildred was married to one of the roughest roughnecks in Oklahoma. He was a big, burly man, and one look at him told you that in his younger days, he was the kind of fellow who didn't step aside for any man. However, around Mildred, he had become quiet and almost gentle. Every time she was hospitalized, Bill practically camped out at the hospital. He would arrive early and stay late.

It was obvious that forty-two years of marriage had created a bond, a closeness between the two. Mildred summed it up one day when she said, "Although we were not blessed with children, we were blessed with each other."

Mildred was the religious one in the family. She had grown up going to church and when she wasn't too weak or too nauseated from her treatments, she still made Bill take her to church. Bill had never been much of a church-goer, but he was willing to take Midred when she felt up to attending. On one occasion, she said, "The only thing good to come out of my illness is that I'm finally getting Bill to church."

On my visits to see Mildred in the hospital, I began to talk with Bill about making a commitment to Christ and the church. At first, I thought I was wasting my time. Bill's response to my inquiries was often anger. He couldn't understand why Mildred, who had lived such a good life, was having to suffer. But, little by little, his attitude began to change. One day he looked at me and said, "Robert, there seems to be a lot of rules to follow and a lot of beliefs to comprehend. Can you make it simple? Can you give me a thumbnail sketch that will explain religion in a nutshell?"

I thought for a moment. How can you explain the beliefs and the doctrines of our faith concisely? Other than just making a long series of statements, how can anyone possibly deal with the complex and essential doctrines of religion in brief? I could recite one of the creeds, like The Apostles' Creed, and say this is what we believe. As a matter of fact, the early creeds came into existence because people were trying to give a short statement of what was important in religion.

However, I thought the creeds might be a little too much for Bill to digest and understand. So, I said, "Bill, you have asked a very good question. It is a question that people have asked for centuries. In fact, it was a question that was put to Jesus. So, the best response I could give to you is tell you what Jesus said. He said:

> . . . *Love the Lord your God with all your heart, with all your soul, with all your mind, and with all your strength . . . and love your neighbor as you love yourself."*

Bill must have understood it because a few weeks later, he walked down the aisle of the church, and confessed his faith and was baptized into the faith.

We live in a world that has become complicated in many ways. Times have changed and people have changed. But, the response that Jesus gave to the question, "What is the greatest commandment?'' is still clear and uncomplicated. For Jesus, religion in a nutshell was loving God with an undivided heart and loving your neighbor as you loved yourself.

As we look at this idea of "religion in a nutshell," I want to examine some ideas and how they apply to our lives.

I. Religion in a nutshell affirms that there is a God. When Jesus was asked, "Which is the greatest commandment?'' he quoted from a familiar Hebrew text (Deuteronomy 6:4-5):

Hear, O Israel, the Lord thy God is one. You shall love the Lord thy God with all of your heart, and with all of your soul, and with all of your mind, and with all of your strength.

This is the basic creed of the Jewish people. It is the first scripture that every Jewish child commits to memory. It is the first sentence with which a service of worship begins in a Jewish synagogue. It is the phrase which the devout Jew wore on a leather bracelet when he went to prayers. When Jesus quoted this phrase as the greatest commandment, the Jews were nodding their heads in agreement. They knew these words meant that we must give our total love to God.

When you are trying to form a clear and concise definition of religion, this is where you start — with loving God. I wouldn't know where else to begin. Belief in and love of God are the basic ingredients, the foundations in any definition of religion.

Several years ago, an architect was given an enormous and almost impossible task. He was to design and build the Imperial Hotel in Tokyo, Japan. Because Japan is a country that frequently experiences tremors and earthquakes, the financial backers wanted a building that would be able to stand up when the quakes came.

No construction job like this had ever been accomplished. The architect was careful and deliberate in drawing his plans. When the core samples were taken where the hotel was to be built, he discovered that eight feet below the surface of the ground lay a sixty-foot bed of soft undisturbed mud. The more he thought about this mud, the more the idea seemed to grow that he could float the foundation of the hotel on this quiet bed of mud.

His theory that the mud would absorb the shocks of the earthquakes was revolutionary. It had never been tried before. After four years of hard work and a lot of jeers and ridicule from skeptical architects and engineers, the building was completed.

Shortly after the Imperial Hotel opened its doors in Tokyo, the worst earthquake Japan had experienced in fify-two years rocked the country. Buildings and houses with strong foundations tumbled and fell into a pile of rubble. But the Imperial Hotel stood firm and strong because the foundation rolled with the shocks of the earthquake.

Religion in a nutshell begins with a foundation that will help absorb some of the shocks of life. The only permanent, enduring foundations in this world are those which are laid according to the plans of the God of eternity. Belief in and love of God are the basic ingredients of any religion. Belief in and love of God form the foundation which enables you to absorb life's most dreadful shocks.

A pastor was called out to a county nursing home to see a woman who wanted to talk to a preacher. She talked with him about her life and she told about having no relatives left. When she became ill, she had no money for care, so she was placed in the county nursing home, She looked at the pastor and said, "It won't be long before you will be called to preach my funeral. When you have the service will you ask someone to sing 'I'm A Child Of The King'?"

When we lay the foundation for our lives in the love of God with all of our hearts, souls, minds, and strength, then we have started with the basic ingredients and we will have no doubt that we are "A Child Of The King."

II. Religion in a nutshell affirms that we are to love our neighbor. After Jesus quoted the scripture as the greatest commandment, he said:

The second most important commandment is this: "Love your neighbor as you love yourself." There is no other commandment greater than these two.

This is also a quote from the Old Testament. It comes from Leviticus 19:18 and in its original context it had to do with other Jews. After all, it was permissible to hate Gentiles. But, Jesus took the old law and widened its meaning to include all people — Jew and Gentile alike.

This broader meaning was a revolutionary idea for Jesus to advocate. He was saying that our love for God must issue in love for our neighbor. And, he was saying that our neighbor is anyone who needs us. A neighbor is anyone who has a need to which you or I have the capacity to respond. We are called to act as a neighbor to every person . . . to those who are hurt . . . to those who are unlovely . . . to those who are outcasts. We are to love people beause they are God's children. After all, how can we love God unless we are willing to love and respond to his people? In other words, we must not allow ourselves to become so hardened that we cannot respond to someone who is in need.

When I was at Drew University in New Jersey, I became friends with a Catholic priest named Sean O'Kelly. Sean was redheaded and always seemed to have a smile on his face and a twinkle in his eyes. He spoke with a heavy Irish brogue because he had only been in America for a few years.

103

While he was in school, he was also pastoring a Catholic church in the heart of Newark, New Jersey. If you want to talk about urban blight and poverty and hunger, all you have to do is to take a trip up and down the streets of Newark.

On one occasion, Sean heard that a family in his parish was hungry. Because of a bureaucratic foul-up, a mother with five small children had no food and no hope of getting any until the end of the month.

Although the family was not Catholic, Sean O'Kelly went to the grocery store and bought a supply of groceries. There were three full sacks, and he went to the apartment building where the family lived. After carrying the groceries up four flights of stairs and walking down a long hall, he came to the apartment. He rang the doorbel!, and a little boy about seven years old answered the door. He looked at Father O'Kelly's clerical collar and the sacks of groceries, and then screamed at his mother: "Mama, Mama, come quick. Jesus brought us some food!"

In telling about that incident, Sean said, "I will never forget that child's comment. At that moment, I realized that I was the Christ for a hungry child."

If we are to be the neighbors that God calls us to be, then we need to understand that you and I are expected to help those we have the capacity to help. The opportunities for service are almost endless in every neighborhood — even yours. There are a dozen ways or more for you to help people if you are willing to be the neighbor God calls you to be! Religion in a nutshell means that you really are expected to be "Jesus" to your neighbors when they are in need.

The last thing I want to say is: *III. Religion in a nutshell, compels us to be his followers.* We have been looking at the commandments. They are a powerhouse of strength and direction of our lives. But, they mean nothing unless we are willing to follow God with our lives.

To those who asked Jesus what the greatest commandment was, he said, "You are not far from the Kingdom of God." We are not far from God's Kingdom, but we must be willing to follow him.

Count Nikolaus Von Zinzendorf had been a very religious fellow in his youth. But, somewhere along the way he had strayed from the faith. He began living in the fast lane, and his faith began to lose its meaning and influence in life.

One day, one of his friends asked him to attend an art show. Together, they walked the corridors of the art gallery until they came to a large painting at the end of the hall.

It was a painting of Jesus hanging on the Cross and the Count studied it very closely. He followed every brush stroke. He looked at the nail prints in the hands and feet. He traced the blood as it trickled down the Master's face from the crown of thorns. He stared at the spear-pierced side. He studied the crucified Christ for a long, long time. Finally, he noticed an inscription at the bottom of the painting. It simply said:

All this I did for thee.
What hast thou done for me?

This was a turning point in the life of the Count. He returned to the faith and became a follower of Christ. And this is what God compels us to do — to be his followers.

So, this is religion in a nutshell.

1. Religion affirms that we are to love God.
2. Religion affirms that we are expected to be a neighbor to anyone in need.
3. Religion compels us to be Jesus' followers.

This is short; this is concise; this is crystal clear.
What will you do about it?

Facing Life's Central Tests

Mark 14:32-42

It was a beautiful spring afternoon in Eastern Oklahoma when my secretary told me that Oleatha was on the phone. Oleatha was sixty-seven years old and she had been having problems. She often became confused. She had a tendency to forget. Once, she had gotten lost going from church out to her home on a bluff that overlooked the lake. At the insistence of her family, she had gone through a battery of medical tests. The reports were in and Oleatha wanted me to come by and visit her.

When I drove into her driveway, I couldn't help but notice the beauty surrounding her home. The redbud trees were blossoming, the tulips had pushed their way up out of the ground and were blooming, and the warm rays of the sun were glistening as they danced across the surface of the lake.

In spite of the beauty of the scenery, I suspected that Oleatha was facing a serious crisis. When I was invited inside her house, I could hear the tea kettle whistling and I knew that she had made me a cup of hot tea because she knew I didn't like coffee. I didn't tell her I didn't care very much for hot tea. As we sat sipping our tea, I asked, "What did the doctors have to say?"

She reached for a tissue and said, "I've told you before about my family history. You know that my mother became mentally incompetent and didn't know anyone or anything for the last three years of her life . . . and you know that my older sister spent the last seven years of her life in a nursing home because she was not mentally competent and didn't know

106

anyone or anything. Well, the doctors now have a name for their diseases. They call it Alzheimers Disease, and they believe that I am in the early stages.''

We were both silent for a moment; then she looked at me and said, "I am so afraid of what lies before me."

This is pretty much the way Jesus felt that night when he shared his last meal with his disciples. When the meal was over, they went out into the dark and deserted streets. Jesus seemed to know where he was going and the disciples trailed along in silent clusters. The only sounds were their sandals clattering along the cobblestone street. They walked past the Lower Pool and through the Fountain Gate. Finally, they headed up a hill toward a garden and the disciples suddenly knew where Jesus was going. He was going to a garden called Gethsemane. They looked back over the city and they could see a few lights twinkling, but most of the people were asleep because it was past midnight. They could see the Temple with its golden spire glistening in the moonlight. In the distance they could hear a Roman sentry calling his watch.

As they stood there looking across the city, they knew that Jesus' life was in danger. It would be so easy for him to slip out of Jerusalem — especially under the cover of night — but they could not persuade him to leave. He seemed to have some kind of rendezvous with destiny, and he refused to listen to their suggestions.

So, while the weary disciples propped themselves up against some olive trees and quickly fell asleep, Jesus wandered off by himself. He knew that his confrontation with the religious authorities had set the die. He knew the possibility of a Roman cross lay before him. And, he was afraid. There, in the stillness of the Garden, he prayed for some other way. He prayed:

Father, all things are possible unto thee; take away this cup from me . . .

107

Fear and doubt had worked their way into the heart and mind of Jesus. He did not want to die! He was only thirty-three years old, and the fear of the Roman cross was real. He had often seen the condemned hanging on crosses outside the city gate. He had heard them moan in pain. He had listened to their curses. He had seen them writhing in agony. Jesus was human, and every bit of his humanity shuddered at the very thought of dying an agonizing death upon a cross. Luke, the physician, describes His fear by saying:

> . . . *and being in agony He prayed more earnestly; and His sweat was as if it were great drops of blood falling down to the ground . . .*

The fear and the doubt glistened in the sweat on his brow as he faced the central test of his life. But, he overcame that doubt as he simply prayed: *" . . . nevertheless, not my will, but thine be done . . ."*

We all face moments like this in our lives. Each of us has prayed to be spared, if possible, some tragedy so real to the imagination that with many of us, day and night, the thought of it is in our minds. We all have those moments when life seems to be closing in. We all have those moments when doubt and fear seem to be getting the best of us. We all have those moments when we feel like we are facing the central tests of life.

A few years ago, I was in New York City on Sunday and went to Riverside Church to hear William Sloan Coffin preach. When he walked into that pulpit, he leaned over it and said, "Here we are again to talk about what is really going on in your soul and mine."

Well, we are talking about what is going on in your soul and mine. We all face tests in life, and we all have a deep desire to be spared. But, we can't be spared the tests of life and we know it. Our challenge is to learn to face the central tests which come our way in life. Next, using the outline of the Gospel, I want to suggest a couple of ways we can face the central tests which come in life.

I. We can face the central tests of life with friends. In that hour when doubt and fear were beginning to crowd in on Jesus, he took his disciples to the Garden of Gethsemane. That reaction makes sense to us. When we are desperate, when life seems to be closing in on us, we like to be with people with whom we feel comfortable. We like to be with people we love and who love us. Jesus wanted to be with his friends, so he took them to the garden. He had twelve disciples, but facing the Cross and the pain of his own fear, he went deeper into the garden with the three men who knew him best — Peter, James, and John.

By this example, Jesus shows us that when things are darkest and life seems to be closing in from all sides, we have a special need for human fellowship. Friends do not have to say much at moments like this; they just need to be people who care. When life seems to be closing in on us, there is nothing more reassuring than being with people who love us.

When I was in seminary, one of my professors was experiencing the sorrow of losing his wife to a terminal illness. Dr. Brown said, "Even though I had told Dorothy Ruth that I would never leave her, my heart trembled at the prospect of being there when she died. On the night of November 7, with death so near, I gently stroked her hair. She opened her eyes and looked at me and said, 'Remember that I love you and I have always loved you.' Then she was gone. There was deep sorrow in my heart at losing my wife of twenty-one years. If anyone had ever felt like his world was closing in on him, it was me."

As the news spread of her death, Dr. Brown said that his friends began to help him through the crisis with their personal visits . . . telephone calls . . . and casseroles. Dr. Brown said, "My dear friends comforted me and strengthened me and loved me. They made me realize once again that God cares and they care. Without the comfort of God and the loving, devoted care of my friends, I doubt that I could have survived the pain of the loss."

Does it sometimes feel like life is closing in on you? Do you feel like you are facing a crisis? a dark period in life? a time of turmoil? Then follow the example of Jesus. When he was facing the Cross, he took his disciples with him. When you sit alone with your friends and share some of your fears, I believe that you will discover strength.

I don't know how many times in counseling situations I have had people tell me their problems. For the first time they share their problems from deep inside with someone else, and they leave saying, "You don't know how much better I feel."

Their problem has not disappeared! They have simply shared their doubts and fears, and they are strengthened because someone knows and cares about them. When you are facing a test, when things seem to be dark and you see no light at the end of the tunnel, when life seems to be closing in on you, remember what Jesus did. He was facing the Cross of Calvary and he went to a Garden called Gethsemane with his disciples — his friends.

II. *We can face the central tests of life when we learn to seek God's fellowship.* Once Jesus was in the Garden, he moved from being with his disciples to being alone with God. He found a place where he could pray — and prayer is communication with God. Each one of us has probably felt a need to pray at some time or another.

One Sunday morning, a Sunday school teacher of eight- and nine-year-old boys and girls suddenly pointed at one little boy and asked, "Bobby, does your family have prayer before breakfast?"

Startled that he had been singled out, Bobby blurted, "No sir, we say our prayers at night! We ain't afraid in the daytime."

This is the pattern that many of us follow — praying or turning to God when we are frightened . . . when we feel life closing in on us . . . when we are facing some test of life. And this is exactly what Jesus did. He could see his path leading to a cross. He was grappling with his life, his very soul; He was praying so intently that he was sweating, as it were, great drops of blood. He was trying to align himself with God. He was seeking God's presence. He was seeking God's fellowship when the worry and doubt and fear began to close in on him.

One of my friends told me about a man in his congregation who had lost both of his sons in a freak accident. As he talked to the grieving father, he asked, "John, how do you feel now?"

The man replied, "I don't feel anything! I'm just numb."

Again the minister asked, "John, how do you feel now?"

The man replied, "I just don't know. I can't see any way out of this terrible loss."

Once more the minister asked, "John, tell me what you really feel like on the inside."

In a voice that was breaking with emotion, John said, "I guess I feel a little like our Lord felt when he said, 'My God, My God, why hast thou forsaken me.' "

The minister smiled and said, "John, I'm not going to worry about you anymore. Any man who seeks to line up his life with God when everything closes in on him knows something about fellowship with God."

All of us have those moments when life closes in on us. All of us have those times when we feel hemmed in by our problems. All of us face those tests in life. And we don't know where to turn. Ultimately, every one of us reaches this point. Even Jesus reached this point in his life, and he responded not by lashing out. He responded not by giving up. He responded not by trying to laugh off his pain. He responded by seeking God's fellowship in prayer.

Is there something in your life that is causing you pain? Is there something in your life that is filling you with doubt and fear? Is there something in your life that seems to have you backed against a wall? Is there some problem that you are facing which seems to have overwhelmed you?

Well, when you are faced with the tests of life, look at what Jesus did that night in the Garden of Gethsemane:

1. He took his disciples with him — his friends who loved and cared about him.
2. He sought God's fellowship in prayer.

If Jesus followed this path when he was faced with the central test of life, shouldn't we follow it, too?

The More Excellent Way

1 Corinthians 13:1-13

The 1988 Winter Olympics were marked by controversy for the U.S. team. The controversy centered around the fact that we had not won as many medals as expected. In fact, the last time we had done so poorly was in 1936.

We won a few medals, and those winners have become household names. Debi Thomas went head to head with the East German, Katerina Witt, and came away with only a bronze medal, Bonnie Blair won the gold medal in speed skating as well as a bronze, Brian Boitano picked up the gold in figure skating, Eric Flaim, Jill Watson, and Peter Oppegard picked up medals for the U.S. Teams, but others who were expected to win medals did not finish in the top three. The hockey team placed seventh — well out of medal contention, the young speed skater named Jensen experienced the tragedy of losing his sister to leukemia on the day of his race and he fell on the ice as he was on his way for the gold, the young girl expected to win the down-hill race was involved in a freak accident, breaking her leg — and could not even compete.

The Olympic woes of the U.S. team at Calgary led to the establishment of a committee to investigate our Olympic training program. George Steinbrenner, owner of the New York Yankees, chaired this committee. In accepting his role on this committee, Steinbrenner said, ''I don't fault the leadership of the U.S. Olympic Committee. We simply must do a better job of developing and preparing U.S. athletes for the future Games. We must strive for excellence on the part of our whole team.''

Just as our Olympic athletes must strive for excellence, I believe that we followers of Jesus Christ must strive for excellence in living the Christian life. We cannot allow our Christian commitment to become a Sunday morning ceremony and ignore it throughout the week. We cannot permit people to think we have the spirit of Christ within our lives when jealousy, and hatred, and greed, and arrogance, and rudeness, and unkindness, seem to be the dominant influences in our lives. We cannot claim to be followers of the carpenter from Nazareth when we do not have an active concern for the good of another person.

In that beautiful hymn of love in 1 Corinthians 13, the Apostle Paul speaks of the method of excellence for the Christian. This is the Apostle Paul at his creative best. This is the Apostle Paul describing the Christian lifestyle in quick phrases, as with light strokes of the brush or pencil. This is the Apostle Paul attempting to describe the more excellent way for the Christian to live. Throughout this magnificent hymn, there are three enduring values which the Apostle Paul says are essential if we are to strive for excellence in living the Christian life. Let's look at these enduring values which Paul describes as the more excellent way.

I. The more excellent way to live includes faith. Faith means different things to different people. But the Apostle Paul is very clear that faith means a commitment to Jesus Christ. It is not enough to believe that he was a good man — though he was. It is not enough to believe that he was a man with high ideals — though he was. It is not enough to believe that he was a great moral teacher — though he was. We must reach that point where we are willing to commit our lives to the One they called Jesus the Christ. Otherwise, we are just going through the motions of religion and there is nothing significant about such a shallow faith. We must discover that One who can make our faith a living, vital faith. But, faith is not something which comes to a person in some magical manner. Faith is something that is discovered. Faith is something that is learned. Faith is something that grows in our hearts and lives.

Malcolm Muggeridge in his book, *Jesus Rediscovered*, described what happened to him when he made a commitment to Jesus Christ. He said:

It was while I was in the Holy land for the purpose of making three BBC television programs on the New Testament that a curious, almost magical certainty seized me about Jesus' birth, ministry, and crucifixion. I became aware that there really had been a man called Jesus who was also God. I was conscious of his presence . . . He really had spoken those sublime words — I heard them . . . He really had died on a cross and risen from the dead . . . Otherwise, how was it possible for me to meet Him as I did? I met Him in the desert wrestling with the Devil . . . I met Him on that hillside preaching of how the meek inherit the earth and the pure in heart see God . . . I met Him falling in step along the road to Emmaus . . . As I tried to explain in my commentary, the words Jesus spoke are living words, as relevant today as when they were first spoken; the light He shone continues to shine as brightly as ever. Thus, Malcolm Muggeridge says, " . . . Jesus is alive . . . The resurrection is historical . . . Jesus is alive . . . The Cross is where history and life . . . legend and reality . . . time and eternity . . . They all intersect at the Cross. There, Jesus is nailed forever to show us how God became a man and a man could become God.

There are many people who need to make the discovery that religion is more than just doing the motions. Religion is more than just acting pious. Religion is more than pretending to be holier than thou. Religion is faith — faith in Jesus Christ. When you have faith in Jesus Christ, you have discovered a more excellent way of living.

II. The more excellent way to live includes hope. You may remember several years ago when Apollo 13 was on its way toward the moon. They were going to be the third group of astronauts to land and walk on the surface of the moon. But, 150,000 miles away from the earth, there was an explosion on board the spacecraft. They were trapped in their ship, they were dangerously low on oxygen, they could not make a U-turn and return to the earth, so they had to continue their journey toward the moon, swing around its dark side, and then head back toward the earth. NASA scientists and technicians began working on plans to make the oxygen supply last long enough to return the astronauts safely to earth. One of the astronauts asked a simple question. He asked, "Is there any hope?"

Hope is not a dreamy, unreal attitude about life. Hope is an essential element if we are ever to achieve any excellence in living. Recently, I went to see the Rogers and Hammerstein play, *South Pacific.* The starring role was played by Robert Goulet. But, because of sickness, the female lead was played by the understudy — and I thought she stole the show. She was vivacious. She was alive. She was enjoying her chance to be a star. At one point in the play, she begins to sing:

I'm stuck like a dope, with a thing called hope.

While that is a lovely attitude, it's not exactly what I mean by hope. This is mostly sentiment. It's like the little boy

116

standing at the window of a pet shop to select a puppy for his birthday present.

The father asks, "Son, have you picked one out yet?"

"Yes, Daddy," said the little boy pointing to a puppy that was wagging his tail furiously. "I want the one with the happy ending."

Hope — a happy ending! This is all that hope means for many people. But the hope that the Apostle Paul talks about is not some shallow or false hope based on sentiment. It is a hope that has been tested in the fires of experience. He encountered persecution; he faced sickness; he was shipwrecked on three occasions; he was beaten and imprisoned. His hope was so sturdy and so real that nothing could shake his confidence, nothing could defeat his faith, nothing could destroy his hope, because his hope was based on Jesus Christ.

In sixteenth-century Britain, a boy was born. Early in life, he was striken by a disease which grotesquely crippled him for life. In spite of his suffering and handicaps, Alexander Pope came to be regarded by many as one of the greatest English poets. This man who knew lifelong suffering wrote: "Hope springs eternal in the human breast."

When you have hope in Jesus Christ, you have discovered a more excellent way of living.

III. The more excellent way to live includes love. Recently, I was reading a biography of the late comedian, Jack Benny. He was married to Mary Livingston for forty-eight years. When he died, he left a provision in his will for a florist to deliver one perfect red rose to Mary every day that she lived.

Our world would be a sadder place in which to live without romantic love. But, the love that the Apostle Paul wrote about is the deepest . . . the most pervasive . . . the most enduring value of the Christian life. The Apostle closed out his great hymn of love by saying:

So faith, hope, love abide, these three; but the greatest of these is love . . .

The supreme expression of love is the way God acts for us in Jesus Christ. He died on the Cross saying this is how much God loves you and me. And, if we are going to discover the more excellent way to live . . . if we are going to have a religion that is alive . . . if we are going to have a religion that is vital and meaningful, then we must have a love that willingly gives to others.

I took my son Jeff to his school late in the afternoon. He is the photographer for the school yearbook and he needed to take a couple of pictures at a basketball game.

While he went into the gym to take his pictures, I sat in the car listening to the 6:00 news on the radio. As I was sitting in the car, I noticed an old woman with two children. One of the children was carrying an empty grocery sack and I watched as they walked over to the big trash dumpster sitting by the corner of the building. They began going through the trash, and I thought they were collecting the cola cans in the dumpster to sell. But they were doing something else . . . something that startled me. They were collecting scraps of food that had been discarded. They were picking up half-eaten sandwiches; they were shaking potato chip bags to see if there were any crumbs left in them; they were salvaging what food they could from the trash dumpster.

Here were three human beings in the shadow of our state capitol and only a stone's throw from our Governor's mansion, and they were getting their food from the garbage. I wanted to help those people and I pulled out my wallet, but the only bill I had was a twenty. I began to rationalize. I began to find excuses to keep my twenty — after all, my wife

Madalyne and I were going out to eat and I would need the money. I began to make excuses about all the money I gave to the church and other missions. Finally, I decided I would go and get some change. And when I looked back over to the dumpster, the old woman and the two children were gone. I guess they had gone around to the other side of the building and I slipped my wallet back into my pocket, ashamed.

I had failed to be the disciple Jesus called me to be. I was condemning myself when all of a sudden, I realized that God was not condemning me. God was using this experience to challenge me. God was challenging me to really think about what it means to be one of his disciples. God was telling me that I may have come up short in what he expects of me, but that I could use this experience to grow spiritually.

All of us have come up short of what God expects of us, but we can be forgiven: we can grow in our commitment; we can discover a more excellent way of living when we try to make love a part of our lives.

Are you trying to find the more excellent way to live?

You can when you make faith . . . hope . . . and love . . . a part of your life.

I Love A Parade

John 12:12-19

Several years ago, while I was pastoring the little Methodist Church in Geary, Oklahoma, a Fourth of July parade was scheduled. Well, there is nothing like a parade in a small town. The entire community gets into the activities. The high school marching band provides the music, there are a few floats, there is a riding club, and even the children are invited to participate by decorating their bicycles and riding in the parade.

Jennifer, my daughter, was five years old and had a bike with training wheels. We spent the morning wrapping streamers through the spokes of her wheels and getting it all decorated so that she could ride it in the parade. She was excited and looking forward to being a part of the activities.

My son Jeff was only three years old and he wanted to be in the parade as well. But, he had one serious problem. He didn't have a bike — not even one with training wheels. However, he did have one of those long green inchworm toys. As he jumped up and down on its back, it would roll down the street. So, we put a couple of streamers on his inchworm, an entry number on Jeff's back, and he was entered in the parade.

All along the parade route, people were pointing out the three-year-old on a green inchworm. They were watching him jump up and down, trying to get his inchworm to keep up with the other children. They were urging him on. They were having a good time watching him take part in the parade. When the prizes were announced, Jeff won second prize in the children's division.

There is something about parades which attracts our attention. Whether we are watching a three-year-old on a green inchworm, or a marching band, we love parades. Perhaps, that is why Palm Sunday has always been a day which catches our attention.

Although Jesus had been avoiding Jerusalem because of his difficulties with the religious leaders, the week of Passover was like a giant magnet which drew him toward the city. Wherever a devout Jew might be, there is a burning ambition within his or her heart to observe the Passover in Jerusalem. Even today, when Jews celebrate the religious holiday of Passover, the say, "This year here; next year Jerusalem."

Like a giant magnet, Jesus was drawn toward the city with the other religious pilgrims. There was an explosive air of expectancy as Jesus made it known that he would be entering the city. A large crowd of people began to gather. In the crowd that day were friends of Jesus — those who followed him, those who had heard him preach, those who had seen him perform miracles, those whose lives had been touched by his.

In the crowd that day were religious pilgrims from around the world. There were people from Judea and Galilee and Egypt and Greece. There were people who had walked across the hills and through the desert so that they might come and spend Passover in the Holy City. The merchants were also in the crowd hawking their wares. They cared nothing for Jesus, except that the large crowd he drew gave them an opportunity to make a little money. The proud Pharisees and the greedy Sadducees were also in the crowd. They were the religious establishment, the hypocrites who always talked about the Lord and on whose lips were ever glib quotations from the Scriptures. They stood in the crowd with their arms folded, disapproving of Jesus and whispering about some way to run him out of town or put him to death.

Yes, the crowds were anxiously waiting as Jesus made his way to Jerusalem. Riding on the back of a donkey, he rode from Bethany along the winding road. When he came to a bend in the road, he could see the tawny walls of Jerusalem just beyond the Kidron Brook. Rising majestically above the walls of Jerusalem was the golden dome of the Temple flashing brilliantly in the morning sun.

As Jesus passed through the city gates and entered the city, a great shout went up from the people:

Hosanna in the highest. Blessed is He who comes in the name of the Lord!

As they shouted, they lined his parade route with palm branches. Visions of the prophets danced in their eyes. Messianic hopes pounded within their breasts. Jesus, riding at the head of the parade, commanded the attention of everyone in the crowd.

The significance of that parade through the streets of Jerusalem is seen in the fact that after 2000 years, we are still remembering it. The shouts have died down, the palm branches have long since withered, the crowds have dispersed and gone their separate ways. But, even today we remember that parade which took Jesus through the streets of Jerusalem.

What was there about that parade that is worth remembering today?

I. The parade into Jerusalem was an act of boldness. Seldom in the history of the world has there been such a display of boldness as Jesus' parade through the streets of Jerusalem. Sometimes we forget that Jesus was an outlaw to the religious authorities of his day. They had already tried to stone him once before.

Common sense should have warned Jesus to stay away from Jerusalem — to stay in Galilee or in the desert. If he absolutely felt that he must go to Jerusalem for the Passover, caution demanded that he enter the city secretly. But Jesus entered the city in such a way that every eye focused upon him. The parade through the Holy City was an act of courage. The parade through the Holy City was a bold claim to be God's Anointed One. The parade through the city was a daring risk to live with a commitment to his faith.

Just as Jesus boldly dared to risk living his faith, we are challenged to risk everything for him. But, somewhere, down through the centuries, we have lost the boldness. In fact, we are often uncomfortable around those who dare to boldly live their faith.

A couple of years ago, I clipped a letter from the Dear Abby column of the paper. The letter was written by a Congregational minister in the Northeast. He began his letter by saying:

One of the toughest tasks a church faces is choosing a good minister. A member of a church undergoing this process lost patience. He had watched the Pastoral Relations Committee reject applicant after applicant for some fault, alleged or otherwise. So, one day he stood up and read a letter from a new applicant.

"Gentlemen," this letter began, "I understand your pulpit is vacant and I would like to apply for the position. I have many qualifications. I have been a preacher with some success and I also have some success as a writer. Some say I am a good organizer. I've been a leader most places I've been. I'm over fifty years of age. I've never preached in one place for more than three years. In some places, I have left town after my work caused riots. I have been in jail on three or four occasions, but not because of any real wrongdoing. My health is not good, though I still get a great deal done. The churches I've preached in have been small, and I'm not too good at keeping records. I have been known to forget whom I have baptized. However, if you can use me, I shall do my best for you.'"

The members of the committee were shocked. Call an unhealthy, troublemaking, absent-minded ex-jailbird as their pastor? That was the most ridiculous thing they had ever heard of and they asked, "Who is the applicant? What is his name?"

The man reading the letter simply smiled and said, "It's signed Paul, an apostle of Jesus Christ."

One of the things that has happened to the church in our day is that Christians have lost their boldness. So often our relationship to God is a casual thing, yet he calls us to be boldly committed to him. He calls us to have the courage to stand up for Christ. He calls us to dare to live our faith.

George Gallup, in his book, *Religion In America*, says that most American Christians never find themselves in moral dilemmas. Not because there are no longer any moral decisions to make, but because we have so watered-down morality that it no longer has any claims upon our lives.

Perhaps, he is right, but our faith still demands boldness. No matter how watered-down we have allowed our faith to get, we are still challenged to have the courage and boldness to live out our faith in Jesus Christ.

I know of a young girl who had always dreamed of attending a prestigious university and pledging a certain sorority. Finally, she reached college and was accepted as a pledge to her chosen sorority.

On her first Sunday at college, she got up and began getting dressed. Her roommate, awakened by the noise, asked what was going on so early. The young girl replied, "I'm getting ready for church."

The shocked roommate sat up in her bed. With complete sincerity she said, "Going to church! You can't be serious! You're a pledge and you'll be black-balled!"

While the girl continued getting dressed, her roommate told her about college students who considered religion to be an immature superstition. She told of the sorority sisters who would not want to be around her. She told of the sorority sisters who would black-ball her from the sorority. The girl was upset at the prospect of being black-balled from her chosen sorority, but she decided that her faith meant more. She went to church and eventually was black-balled from that particular sorority. But, in the process, she gained a deeper and more meaningful faith.

Do you have the courage to stand for your faith?

Do you have the inner strength and boldness to live out your faith?

II. The parade into Jerusalem was an act of humility. A pastor was once asked to speak at a banquet for a charitable organization. After the meeting, the program chairman handed the pastor a check. "Oh, I don't want this," the pastor said. "I appreciate the honor of being asked to speak. Keep the check and apply it to something special."

The program chairman asked, "Well, do you mind if we put it in our special fund?"

"Of course not," the pastor replied. "What is the special fund for?"

The chairman answered, "It's so we can get a better speaker for next year."

Life is full of humbling experiences. But, when we look at Jesus' parade through the Holy City, we sense that it was an act of humility. He did not choose to ride into the city upon a stallion, but a donkey. He was not coming in the might and power of a conquering king, but as a humble servant.

Jesus was using his parade through the Holy City to teach that humility is the key to greatness. The idea of greatness is directly related to being a servant. The one issue which Jesus made abundantly clear is that he came not to be served, but to serve. If we are ever to attain the humility of Jesus, then we must realize that we, too, are called to be servants.

Recently, I read the biography of a man who was one of the most learned people of his generation. He had a Ph.D. in philosophy, he had a Ph.D. in theology, he was a world-class musician, and concert halls around the world were sold out when he went on tour. Then, to the surprise of everyone, he decided he wanted to go back to school. Not to teach as a member of the faculty, but to earn yet another doctoral degree. This third doctorate that he received was in medicine.

As soon as he had his medical degree, he left the comfortable surroundings of Western Europe and went into the jungles of Africa. There he cleared away part of the jungle and began building a clinic and a hospital. Once these were built, he started providing medical care to the young and old of Africa.

Many years later, Dr. Albert Schweitzer won the Nobel Peace Prize for his ministry of healing in the jungles of Africa. When he accepted the Nobel Peace Prize, he shared with that distinguished crowd in Stockholm the reason he had built a hospital in Africa. The reason was summed up, he stated in the first words he always said to his native patients as they awakened from an operation. He would say: "The reason that you have no more pain is because the Lord Jesus told the good doctor and his wife to come to the banks of Ogooue River and help you. If you owe thanks to anyone, you owe it to the Lord Jesus.''

He accepted the challenge to humbly be a servant of Jesus Christ. And this is our challenge — this is *your* challenge — this is *my* challenge! Look beyond your needs to the needs of others and you will be on the road to being a humble servant of Jesus Christ.

Someone put it so simply long ago when he said:

Find a hurt and heal it;
Find a need and fill it.

When we do this, we are on the road to being humble servants of Jesus Christ.

When you do this, you are on the road to discovering greatness as one of the followers of Jesus Christ.

The Richest Hill On Earth

John 19:16-37

All of us have taken trips that were memorable. There are certain vacations that stick in our minds. Perhaps, we were lying on a beach on a tropical island. Perhaps, the crisp cold wind was whipping against our face as we skied down the side of a mountain. Perhaps, we simply curled up with a good book and forgot about our everyday routines. We all have memories of certain trips or vacations that are as clear today as they were when we took them.

Many years ago, I was with my family on vacation in Montana. We were driving along a road that was winding among the hills and valleys when we suddenly rounded a sharp curve and saw a large, barren mountain right in front of us. There were no trees on the side of this mountain. It was scarred from years of being mined. It was a desolate, deserted mountain with a large sign which proclaimed, "This is the richest hill on earth."

Perhaps, you have guessed by now that this was Silver Bow Mountain. Since 1876, more wealth has been mined from this mountain than from any other mountain on earth. First silver was discovered, and that's how it was named Silver Bow Mountain. Then gold was discovered and later, copper was mined from this mountain. Since 1876, the mines in Silver Bow Mountain have yielded over thirteen billion pounds of silver, gold, and copper. In today's market prices, billions and billions and billions of dollars of wealth have been taken out of the mountain, which makes its claim as the richest hill on the earth a valid claim.

However, in spite of the wealth that has come out of Silver Bow Mountain, I believe that there is another hill which can lay claim to being "the richest hill on earth." This other hill was called Calvary, and it was on this hill where Jesus was crucified. This is an historical fact! Jesus was arrested and went through the mockery of a trial. Pilate tried to find some reason to release Jesus, but when the crowd kept chanting, "Crucify . . . Crucify . . ." he washed his hands of involvement and then handed Jesus over to be beaten and crucified. Jesus was led down the road — staggering under the weight of the Cross.

The crowds gathered to watch the side show which took place just outside the city gates. The religious people were there! The greedy Sadducees and the proud Pharisees were standing there with their arms folded approvingly as the nails were driven through Jesus' flesh. The friends of Jesus were there! There was Mary, the mother of Jesus, and Mary and Martha, and his disciples — Peter, James, John, Andrew, Thomas, Matthew, Phillip, Bartholomew, and all the rest watching with grief in their hearts. The sightseers came to gawk, and a few entrepreneurs worked the crowd hawking their wares. There they stood — watching as Jesus was crucified! He hung on the Cross for almost six hours before he died.

To be honest, this crucifixion seemed to be no different than any other crucifixion. After all, crucifixions were fairly common in that day. There was nothing pretty about a crucifixion; there was nothing romantic about a crucifixion; there seemed to be nothing religiously significant about Jesus dying on the Cross. Yet, everything about the crucifixion of Jesus was sad and heartbreaking.

And now, his crucifixion at Calvary has become a central part of the history of our world. Calvary has become the richest hill on earth because it has showed us something new about God.

129

As we look at the Cross of Calvary once again, let us examine how Calvary enables us to see some realities about God. *I. Calvary is the richest hill on earth because it revealed the nature of God.* Recently at one of our Annual Conferences, Bishop John Russell of the Dallas/Fort Worth area was our conference preacher. John had served most of his ministry in Oklahoma and he was invited back to speak. In one of his sermons, he told of an event that had taken place shortly after he had assumed his office as Bishop. He was invited to have lunch at a downtown office building with a man he had never met. The man told Bishop Russell that his secretary would meet him in the lobby of the building and bring him up to his office. Bishop Russell knew that he would not recognize the secretary and simply assumed that she would recognize him. He arrived a little early and sat down to wait in the lobby. After a while, he noticed a woman walking around the lobby as though she were looking for someone. She walked over to him and asked, "Do you, by chance know Bishop Russell?"

He decided he would have a little fun and replied, "Yes, I know Bishop Russell."

She asked, "When you see him, will you tell me?"

He said that he would, and the woman turned to look around the lobby once more. Then, looking at him again, she asked, "Since you know Bishop Russell, would he be the kind of person who would be late?"

He smiled and replied, "No, I don't believe the bishop would be late at all. If anything, I think he would be early."

She thanked him, and he began to wonder how he was going to stop this little charade. He decided that he had better tell her that he was Bishop Russell. He looked at her and said, "This started off as a joke, but now I feel silly. I'm Bishop Russell."

She looked surprised and asked, "You are? Well, I'll tell you one thing, you don't look like a bishop."

And he asked, "What does a bishop look like?"

And she said, "How should I know? I'm a Baptist."

Just as the Bishop finally had to reveal who he was, it was the Cross of Calvary which revealed the true nature of God. Before Jesus, God was a theological concept; before Jesus, God was a power that demanded adherence to the law; before Jesus, God was a mysterious God confined to the Temple in Jerusalem. But Jesus came and was crucified. It was on the Cross of Calvary where Jesus bled and died to say to us, "God is like this."

That is the Gospel! The crucifixion of Jesus on the Cross of Calvary said to the whole world, "God is like I am." Spit on him, he doesn't spit back . . . slap him, he doesn't slap back . . . crucify him, he doesn't crucify you . . . curse him, he doesn't curse you . . . kill him, he doesn't kill you.

Almost two thousand years have come and gone, but the rains of the centuries have not washed away his blood from the rotting wood of a deserted cross, nor have the winds of time swept away his footprints from along the shore of Galilee. The Cross still stands at Calvary as the truth which reveals to us the real nature of God. The Good News is that God is like Jesus.

II. Calvary is the richest hill on earth because it revealed the compassion of God. For me, one of the central revelations of the Cross is the depth of God's love for us in spite of what we are. His love will not be discouraged by our sins. The Apostle phrased it so simply: *"While we were yet sinners Christ died for us . . ."* We do not have to earn God's love. The Cross of Calvary reminds us that we can never be worthy of God's love, yet his love is always available to us.

131

Most of us can identify with the little boy who had been giving his mother a bad time all day. Finally, she had had enough and sent him to bed early. As he was saying his prayers, he prayed, "Dear God, please love me even when I am bad."

This is not only our prayer, but it is our hope. People may say they are through with us, our friends may reject us, society may give up on us, but the God we see revealed in the Cross of Calvary will do none of these things, because he loves us. We may not deserve his love, but he continues to love us.

I was reading a story recently about the great Alabama football coach, Bear Bryant. Alabama was playing several years ago in the Cotton Bowl on New Year's day. Alabama was holding a three point lead in the final minutes of the fourth quarter. Alabama punted the ball; the receiver caught it and took off running down the sidelines. He was on his way to a touchdown.

The players on the Alabama bench were standing and urging their teammates on the field to stop him. All of a sudden, one of the players on the Alabama bench, overcome by excitment, ran out onto the field and made a beautiful tackle. Then, he jumped up and ran back over to his bench and sat down, as if no one had seen him. Of course, thousands of people in the stands and millions of people on national television had seen him.

A touchdown was awarded to the opposing team, and the tackler sat on the bench with his head down. He could no more explain what he had done than we can explain some of the foolish things we have done. But, his mistake was in front of 75,000 people in the stadium and millions of people watching on television.

Some of the people in the stands began to scream, "Throw him out!" And that was one of the nicer things they said. The young man just sat there, hanging his head in shame. Then the whole stadium seemed to grow quiet. Coach Bear Byrant went over and sat on the bench beside the player. He put his arm around his shoulder as though to say, "You made a mistake, but you are still a part of the team."

That is God's message to us through the Cross of Calvary. he is saying, "I forgive you"; he is saying, "I love you"; he is saying, "There is nothing you can do which will separate you from my love."

And that is God's compassion. In spite of who we are or what we do, God's love and compassion is with us because the Cross of Calvary tells us there is not anything in this world that stands between us and God. There is nothing that will separate us from God. There is nothing that will keep God from loving us. There is nothing that can stop his love for you and me.

III. Calvary is the richest hill on earth because it reveals God's power. When we speak of the power of God, we often get lost in childish concepts and argue about whether or not it means that God is going to do something miraculous or magical. Sometimes we think the power of God means that anything that happens to us is the direct result of his will or desire. But, of course, there are thousands of things which happen to us every day that are the direct result of our free choices . . . our ignorance . . . or our stupidity.

Perhaps a more mature understanding of the power of God is revealed in the Cross of Calvary. The Apostle Paul, living in a world that equated power with brute force and military might, seemed to delight in preaching the Cross of Calvary as the power of God. It may have been a foolish tale to the Greeks and a stumbling block to the Jews, but Paul said:

For the preaching of the cross . . .
is the power of God . . .

He was aware that the idea of a serving, suffering God was an absurdity in the world of Caesar. The only sin to a Roman was to be weak. Yet, Paul saw with clear insight that God was using the Cross of Calvary to save men and women . . . to change their hearts . . . and to win their wills to his.

There are only two kinds of power in the area of human relationships. One is *coercion* or power *over* people. The other is *persuasion* or power *with* people. In the long run, coercion never works because force is always destructive.

Long ago, Napoleon was imprisoned on the island of St. Helena. He became reflective one day and said, "Alexander, Caesar, Charlemagne, and myself have founded empires. Upon force we founded them and they are gone. Jesus Christ alone has founded his empire upon love, and at the very hour millions would die for him whom they have never seen."

The power of God is revealed in the Cross of Calvary. It is a power more real than all the massed armies in the world. It is a power that could smash us. It is a power that could force us. It is a power that could compel us to reach out to him. But, instead it is God reaching out to us and letting us know very simply that he loves us!

We may not completely understand how Calvary reveals God's power, but it is God's plan for salvation. And I don't think God has another plan.

Seeing Jesus on the Cross of Calvary, we come to know God's love and God's power for our lives. Have you made this discovery of God's love and God's power in your life?

The Easter Event — After The Resurrection

Matthew 28:1-10

A community wide Easter pageant was planned, and people from all over the county tried out for various parts. The part of Mary Magdalene was given to a Catholic nun, a local doctor became Peter, a high school principle became Judas, and Caiphais, the hypocritical high priest, was played by a local banker. It was relatively easy selecting the people for the various parts in the Easter pageant. However, the part of Jesus was difficult to cast. No one seemed to fit the director's idea of what Jesus would be like — no one, that is, except for the most unlikely charcter, a big, burly oil field worker. But, he was out of the question. How could the director select someone to play the part of Jesus who cursed like a sailor and had a reputation for barroom brawls? But he was the one she chose, because he was the logical choice.

Finally, the day of the Easter pageant arrived and people from all over the state came to see the performance. There must have been ten thousand people gathered on the hillside to watch the dramatic re-enactment of the last week in the life of Jesus.

When they came to that part of the play where Jesus was led away to be crucified, one little man who was simply filling in as an extra as a part of the crowd, became caught up in the emotion of the part, he joined in on the shouts of "Crucify!" . . . "Crucify!" . . . "Crucify!." As Jesus was being led away toward Calvary, carrying the Cross on his back, he

135

walked past this little man in the crowd, who was still caught up in the emotion of the moment, shouting insults at the top of his voice. Just as the character playing Jesus walked by, this little man spit in his face. The big, burly man stopped in his tracks. He reached up and wiped his face dry, looked at this little man, and said, "I'll be back to take care of you after the Resurrection."

The events that took place after the Resurrection are what have made this day called Easter so special. Mary Magdalene and the other Mary certainly did not expect anything special. After all, they had seen Jesus die on that Roman Cross. Now, as the light was dawning on the eastern horizon, they made their way toward his tomb to complete the anointing of his body. The only thing that they were expecting was the bleak, cold reality of death. But, when they arrived at the tomb, they were surprised at what they discovered. The tomb was open, the stone rolled away, the body of Jesus gone. The burial clothes were lying on the stone in the shape of a body, collapsed and slightly deflated, like a glove from which the hand has been removed. According to the story, an angel of the Lord said to the women:

Fear not, for I know that you seek Jesus, who was crucified. He is not here: for He is risen from the dead.

The women then left the tomb, and they encountered the risen Christ. He was alive!

And that is the Easter Event. It is a true story, the narrative of an experience relayed in several ways by the Gospel writers. Mary Magdalene and the disciples and all of the others were overwhelmed with the Easter Event. They did not expect it; it was not a figment of their imaginations; it was a reality — Jesus was alive!

This is a story that is simple, yet profound. I don't completely understand it, but I believe it with everything in my being. I really don't know what I would preach if I didn't believe in the Resurrection of Jesus. I believe it because of the difference it makes in your life and mine.

Now, there are two ideas which I think were prevalent after the Resurrection.

I. After the Resurrection, there was disbelief. When the women were first told of the Resurrection, there was disbelief. They thought someone had stolen the body of Jesus. All they wanted was to anoint his body with ointments so that he could have a proper burial. They had trouble believing the Resurrection at first.

When the women ran back to the Upper Room and told the disciples the news of the Resurrection, there was disbelief there as well. Peter and John wanted to find out what had really happened, and they went running to the empty tomb.

When Jesus appeared to the disciples in the Upper Room, Thomas was not there. He was off grieving in his own way, and he missed the encounter with the risen Lord. When the others told him of their experience, there was disbelief. Thomas simply said, "I didn't see him. Unless I see him for myself, I will not believe."

Unfortunately, many of us are imprisoned by disbelief. We may not say with our lips, "I will not believe." But, we say it by the way we live our lives. We are filled with loneliness. We are filled with despair. We feel that our lives don't matter. We live as if we do not believe, because we live as if we do not need God's help or anyone's help.

One Saturday morning, I saw a look of disbelief on my wife's face. It was one of those cold, snowy Saturday mornings and I had just told her I would make breakfast by myself. She looked skeptical. I'm not sure if she just didn't believe her ears or if she was afraid to leave me in the kitchen alone.

I decided that the perfect breakfast on a cold morning would be cream of wheat, juice, and toast. Now, when I say toast, I'm not talking about that whimpy way of using a toaster; I'm talking about making toast the way it should be made. You slap a lot of butter on some bread and stick it in the oven to broil. When you take it out, it is just dripping with melted butter.

Unfortunately, after putting the toast in the oven, I got busy with other things. In fact, I didn't remember the toast again until the smoke alarm went off. You know, smoke alarms are a pretty good way to call everyone to the kitchen. My wife and both kids came to see what was going on. I shooed them out because I had everything under control all by myself. I have a suspicion that my wife called the fire department and told them, "Don't worry, my husband's just cooking breakfast."

I was trying to do something on my own and I wasn't doing too well. And this is the way we are in life. We may not say we don't believe, but we live as though we don't believe. We try to make it through life on our own. We try to live as though we don't need God. And our lives end up in a mess.

On that first Easter, each one of those followers experienced the presence of the risen Lord. Suddenly, they knew that he was there. Suddenly, they knew that he cared. Suddenly, they knew that he was alive. Suddenly, they knew that they were not alone anymore, and their belief turned to faith.

You may have been trying to make it on your own in life and yet been filled with loneliness. You may be filled with despair. You may feel like things are dark and bleak. But, if you will simply open the eyes of faith, I believe that you, too, can experience the risen Lord. When you do, you will discover a God that cares about you.

II. After the resurrection, there was a joyful hope. When the women went to the tomb, there was sorrow in their hearts. They were thinking about the task which lay before them. They had to anoint the body, but how would they roll away the stone? But, when they arrived, the stone is rolled away, the body of Jesus is missing, and an angel tells them, "He is not here; he is risen . . ." Then, Matthew says they left the tomb "filled with joy." But, the joy they felt was more than simple happiness; it was a joy that was filled with hope. The joyful hope that came alive in those First Easter Christians was that Jesus was resurrected from the grave — and they would be conquerors of the grave as well.

The joyful hope of conquering death brought the disciples out of hiding and sent them into the world proclaiming the good news of the Easter event. They were changed people because they knew that God had not deserted them. The Apostle Paul proclaimed this joyful hope when he wrote to the Roman church:

> *I am convinced that nothing can separate us from the love of God — nothing in death or life, nothing in all of creation will be able to separate us from Christ Jesus our Lord.*

There is an old story which depicts in a humble way the joyful hope that the Resurrection brings to our hearts and lives. The story is about a young boy named John Todd who was born in Vermont in October 1880. Before long, his family moved to the small community of Killingworth, Connecticut. Shortly before he was six years old, he was ophaned by the death of his parents. The children in the home were parceled out among their relatives. John was assigned to live with a kindhearted aunt who lived about ten miles aways. She was father

and mother to him. She raised him and helped him through
Yale University.

Years later, the aunt became seriously ill and knew that
she was close to death. She was afraid to die, and uncertain
about the experiences she had to face. She wrote to her nephew
and told him of the fears in her heart. John Todd replied to
his aunt with a letter which said:

*It is now thirty-five years since I, a little boy of six, was
left alone in the world. I have never forgotten the day
when I made the long journey to your house in North
Killingworth. I still recall my disappointment when, instead of coming for me yourself, you sent your hired
man, Caesar, to fetch me. And I can still remember my
tears and anxiety, as perched high on your horse and
clinging tightly to Caesar, I started out for my new
home. As we rode along and night fell, I became more
afraid. "Do you think she'll go to bed before I get
there" I asked Caesar anxiously.*

*"Oh, no," he answered reassuringly. "She will be
sure to stay up for you. When we get out of these woods,
you will see her candle shining in the window."*

*Presently, we did ride into a clearing, and there, sure
enough, was your candle. I remember you were waiting at the door . . . that you put your arm around me
. . . that you lifted me down from the horse . . . there
was a fire on your hearth . . . and a warm supper on
your stove . . . After supper, you took me up to bed,
heard my prayers, and then sat beside me until I dropped
asleep.*

*You undoubtedly realize why I am recalling these
things. Some day soon God may send for you, to take
you to a new home. Don't fear the summons . . . the*

strange journey . . . or the messenger of death
. . . At the end of the road, you will find love and a
welcome waiting for you . . . you will be as safe there
as you are here . . . you will be in God's love and care
. . . Surely God can be trusted to be as kind to you as
you were years ago to me.

This is the joyful hope of the Easter Event. I do not completely understand the mystery of the Resurrection. I have no answer for "why" and "how" he walked out of that tomb alive. But, I believe that he did it! I believe that the tomb is open. I believe that Jesus is alive. And because he lives, I am here to tell you that the most exciting thing in the world is that you live, too!

This is the Gospel message — Jesus lives and so will you!

Five Minutes After Death

There is an old Arab parable about a merchant in Bagdad who sent his servant to the market one day. Before very long, the servant returned, white and trembling with fear. There was great agitation in his voice as he said: "Master, down in the market place I was jostled by someone in the crowd. When I turned around, I saw that it was Death who had jostled me. She looked at me and made a threatening gesture. Master," he said, "please lend me your horse, for I must hasten away to avoid Death. I will ride to Samara and there I will hide, and Death will be unable to find me."

The merchant lent his horse and the servant galloped away in a great hurry. Later, the merchant went down to the market place and saw Death standing in the crowd. He went over to Death and asked: "Why did you frighten my servant this morning? Why did you make a threatening gesture?"

"That was not a threatening geture," Death replied. "It was only a start of surprise. I was astonished to see him here in Bagdad, for I have an appointment with him tonight in Samara."

Each of us has an appointment in Samara. We all realize that death is a realistic fact that comes to everyone. It comes to the king in his palace . . . to the beggar beside the road . . . and to the animal hiding in its hole.

But what happens to us after death? Are we like candles blown out in the wind? What happens to us after this life?

I visited a young man who had suffered with a terminal illness for quite some time. He was in the hospital intensive

142

care unit for well over 100 days. I suppose that he was hooked up to almost every machine known to medical science. His total existence during that 100 days was that small eight by ten room in the intensive care unit.

Most of the time, communciation with him was difficult. He was on a respirator to assist his breathing, and he could not talk. All that he could do was shake his head up and down for "yes" or right to left for "no."

On a few occasions, when I went to see him, he was off the respirator and breathing on his own. During these short periods, he was able to speak. Once, as we were talking, he looked at me and said, "Robert, I know it is just a matter of time until I die. I've come to terms with that and death no longer frightens me. But, what happens next? What happens to us five minutes after death?"

What happens five minutes after death? This is a question which has been in the hearts and minds of people since the beginning of time. We want to get a glimpse across the threshold, so that the unknown will not be so frightening. We have no blueprint which enables us to know very clearly what happens five minutes after we cross the threshold of death. All that we possess are the promises of our faith . . . the lovely language of imagery . . . the beautiful phraseology of pictures. The New Testament only gives us appetizing hints about the life to come. In the twenty-first chapter of Revelation, the writer said:

And I saw a new heaven and a new earth: for the first heaven and the first earth were passed away: and there was no more sea. And I, John, saw the holy city, new Jerusalem, coming down from God out of heaven . . .

That is a vivid allusion! But, it is still only an allusion; it is still only a picture; it is still only an imagery; and it leaves so much to the imagination. Perhaps this is exactly what God intended. Perhaps it is enough for us to believe in a Savior who has gone to prepare a place for us. The Apostle Paul, attempting to sum up his thoughts of what will happen to us in the world to come, said:

> . . . *The eye has not seen, nor the ear heard, neither have entered into the heart of man, the things which God has prepared for them that love him . . .(1 Corinthians 2:9)*

Instead of trying to claim any personal insight into what will happen five minutes after death, I want to lift up some of the great images of our faith.

I. Five minutes after death there will be no more pain or sorrow or hurting. There will be grieving in the hearts and lives of those left behind. When we lose someone whom we love, there is a vacant spot left in our hearts . . . an aching within our lives . . . a sorrow that never really goes away.

There was a letter to the editor in the local paper that was very touching. A mother wrote the letter because that day would have been her son's eighteenth birthday. One year ago he had been killed in a tragic incident, and she was writing to express the pain she still felt. She was writing to express how the sorrow would come out of the blue and tears would fill her eyes. She was writing to express the grief she felt when she thought of a seventeen-year-old boy who never got a chance to fulfill his potential.

Most of us know something of what she was talking about. We have lost those we love, and the sorrow and pain is very real. But the promise of the writer of Revelation is that five minutes after death there will be life that will never end

. . . a life of beauty and peace and love . . . a life in which there will be no more pain . . . no more sorrow, nor tears . . . nor crying . . . nor parting . . . nor death after death. This is the eternal hope of the New Testament.

I stood once by the side of a bed in one of our hospitals where an old man lay dying. He was racked with pain and had difficulty breathing. As he looked up into my face, he held my hand tightly. He was so weak . . . so frail . . . that I was surprised at the stength with which he held on to my hands. In a voice that tembled with emotion, he said: "There are so many things we don't understand. I don't know why the Lord lets us suffer like this, but I know I won't be suffering much longer. I know that everything will be all right because I'm going home . . . I'm going home . . . and I wish I were there now . . ."

And he was right! In just a short time, he crossed over that threshold and went to that place where he did not have to suffer anymore. He went to that place where he did not have to struggle for a breath of air. He went to that place that was promised by Jesus. He went to enjoy the rest and peace and joy of those who die in the Lord.

II. *Five minutes after death there will be a reunion with loved ones.* The promise of Jesus to the thief on the cross was very clear: *"Today, you will be with me in paradise."* They were suffering in this world together. But when they went into the next, they not only would not be suffering, but they would be together. This I believe, is at the very heart of the Gospel . . . the promise of a reunion . . . the promise that we will be together again . . . the promise that death cannot eternally separate us from those we love.

Do you believe that right now? Do you believe that God will never allow a life to slip through his fingers? If you believe that, then you know that the hope for a reunion with those loved ones who have gone before you is not something utterly insane.

When I was in high school, there were four teenage girls killed in a car wreck. The four girls had been to Dallas and they were coming home late that evening. They were traveling on a new highway that was still under construction in a few sections. Apparently, as a practical joke, someone removed the barriers where a bridge was to be built over the Trinity River. The first driver that came along was able to slam on his brakes and stop his car just before he went over the edge of the cliff and down into the river.

The man who stopped his car saw another car coming; he jumped out of his car and tried to flag it down to stop them before they went over the edge. But, the four girls must have been frightened when they saw the man trying to get them to stop. Instead of slowing down, they speeded up and sailed over the edge of the cliff. All four girls were killed instantly.

A shock-wave of grief and sorrow swept over that community. High school students — who believed that they were invincible — were suddenly confronted with the deaths of four of their own. We had seen grandparents pass away, we had seen graphic pictures of car wrecks on the news and in our Driver's Education classes, but, there was not a one of us who had really believed it could happen to us.

Along with a large group of other students, I went to the funeral services. Even though better than twenty years have passed since that spring afternoon, I still remember the Episcopal priest looking out at the families and saying in a very gentle voice, "I know that you are hurting right now. But, I can assure you that these girls are not gone forever. I know that you will see your daughters once again. You will be reunited with them one day."

I have no documentary evidence to support such a hope. There is no way to prove what happens to us at death. I realize now, as surely as he did then, that philosophical and theological hope must support such an assertion of faith. But, I want you to know that in the sanctuary of my soul, I believe that the hope and promise of our faith is that five minutes after death there will be joy and happiness throughout the heavens as we are reunited with those loved ones who have gone before us.

III. Five minutes after death we will be in the presence of God. I believe with everything that is within me that we are in the presence of God right now. Across the centuries, no experience has been more universal than the sense of Someone greater than ourselves dwelling with us. However, no one has ever seen the presence of God. But no one has ever seen an idea . . . No one has ever seen the truth . . . No one has ever seen a thought . . . No one has ever seen love . . . We haven't seen them, but we know they exist. The deepest forces of our lives can't be seen, but they are real. It is the same with the presence of God. We can't see his Divine Presence, but it is real.

There is a lot which we do not understand about death and eternal life. But when death comes, why should death sever that tie binding our spirits to God? It doesn't! Death does not separate us from God's presence. Death simply makes his presence more real to us!

I believe that five minutes after death, we will be in the presence of God. We will be resting in the bosom of Jesus.

If you have committed your life to Jesus Christ, this belief . . . this hope . . . can be yours.